Routledge Revivals

I0025549

Contemporary Britain

First published in 1971, *Contemporary Britain* presents lectures by Barbara Wootton, well known as a socialist and agnostic and her opinions habitually run counter to those of the political Right and occasionally also to those of the Left. In these lectures she surveys the state of the nation from the angle of her personal philosophy, in a wide-ranging review which covers, amongst other topics, collective bargaining and incomes policy; legislation on abortion, censorship and gambling; the validity of opinion polls; the rise in crime, the decline in religious belief, and the need to popularize a secular morality based only on consideration for others.

Incisively written and infused with a warm humanity, this book will be an interesting read for students of British politics and political science in general.

Contemporary Britain

Three Lectures

Barbara Wootton

Routledge
Taylor & Francis Group

First published in 1971
by George Allen & Unwin Ltd.

This edition first published in 2024 by Routledge
4 Park Square, Milton Park, Abingdon, Oxon, OX14 4RN

and by Routledge
605 Third Avenue, New York, NY 10017

Routledge is an imprint of the Taylor & Francis Group, an informa business

© George Allen & Unwin Ltd, 1971.

Publisher's Note
The publisher has gone to great lengths to ensure the quality of this reprint but points out that some imperfections in the original copies may be apparent.

Disclaimer
The publisher has made every effort to trace copyright holders and welcomes correspondence from those they have been unable to contact.

A Library of Congress record exists under LCCN: 77873925

ISBN: 978-1-032-75249-5 (hbk)
ISBN: 978-1-003-47308-4 (ebk)
ISBN: 978-1-032-75250-1 (pbk)

Book DOI 10.4324/9781003473084

CONTEMPORARY BRITAIN

THREE LECTURES
BY
BARBARA WOOTTON

London
GEORGE ALLEN & UNWIN LTD
RUSKIN HOUSE MUSEUM STREET

Printed in Great Britain
in 12 pt. Fournier type
by Cox and Wyman Ltd
London, Fakenham and Reading

NOTE

These lectures were delivered in October 1970. With the rapid movement of events, some of what was then said was already out of date at the time of going to press. Wherever possible, I have done my best to bring the original text up to date.

B. W.

December 1970

CONTENTS

1

THE AFFLUENT, ACQUISITIVE
PERMISSIVE SOCIETY

I

To anyone associated with the Humanist or Secularist Movement anywhere in the world, the opportunity to deliver a
course of lectures in commemoration of Voltaire must be
regarded as at once an honour and a responsibility. I wish,
therefore, at the outset to express my appreciation to the
British Humanist Association as organizers of this course for
their invitation to myself, to University College for generously
providing the necessary accommodation and to Lord Annan
for presiding at the first lecture.

Two adjectives are frequently applied to contemporary
Western societies. The first is 'affluent' and the second 'permissive'. To these I would add a third – 'acquisitive' – which in
my view describes an even more dominant characteristic of the
world in which we live. In this first lecture I propose to discuss
to what extent and in what sense the use of these epithets is an
accurate description of the present British way of life, and to
examine what changes in outlook and behaviour have accompanied, whether as cause or effect, increasing affluence and increasing permissiveness in a persistently acquisitive society. In
this decision to confine myself to British experience the over-

riding factor has been the wish to present evidence as well as conclusions: had I stretched the canvas further, considerations of space and time would have made it necessary to spread the paint very thinly. It is, however, common knowledge that the social histories of many Western industrial communities have followed broadly similar courses, though always with local variations of detail: much of what is said, therefore, should have a wider application.

To begin with affluence. In purely monetary terms, most of us are certainly richer than we were even ten years or so ago. Between 1959 and 1967 the number of (pre-tax) incomes below £600 p.a. fell from 15,500,000 to 9,362,000, a drop of nearly 40 per cent: the number between £600 and £2,000 rose from 10,475,000 to 16,578,000, an increase of over 58 per cent; and the number from £2,000 upwards rose from 525,000 to 1,860,000, an increase of no less than 254 per cent. Nor do these figures merely reflect the falling value of money. On the contrary, the changing pattern of consumption makes it clear that every year the great British public (or a conspicuous section thereof) is growing richer and richer. In the ten years from 1956 to 1966 expenditure on the purchase of motor-cars and cycles (at 1958 prices) rose from £282 million to £935 million, that is by 231 per cent: on drink by nearly 34 per cent from £899 million to £1,204 million; on entertainments and recreation by 36 per cent from £275 million to £374 million; while consumers' expenditure overseas, mainly foreign travel, rose by about 53 per cent from £217 million to £333 million. By contrast, outlay on food has increased by a mere 14 per cent from £3,963 million to £4,527 million.[1]

In the past two years the pace of wage and salary increases

[1] Source: Central Statistical Office, National Income and Expenditure (HMSO 1967 and 1969).

has greatly accelerated; and, in spite of the comparable accelera-
tion of retail price rises, it would seem that at least up to the
summer of 1970 real standards were still rising. In the average
(but by no means in everybody's) budget, cars, drink, entertainments and holidays abroad are absorbing an increasing, and
plain necessities such as food a diminishing, proportion of the
total.

Not less remarkable than this swelling tide of affluence is the
change in public attitude and public expectation. Since the end
of the war it has become accepted, almost as a law of nature,
that everybody's (or nearly everybody's) income should move
regularly upwards. In periods of extreme stringency there may
indeed be occasional episodes of severe restraint, or even total
freeze; but these are regarded as deplorable exceptions to the
normal upward trend. Yet how many people realize how recent
is the origin of this assumption? You do not need to go back
further than the nineteen-thirties to find that wages and
salaries, far from being regularly increased, were actually subject to frequent and substantial reductions. 'Not a penny off the
pay not a minute on the day' was the battle-cry of those days.
I myself worked for the University of London, for ten years
immediately before Hitler's war, for an entirely static salary
without any advance or even annual increment; and this was
nothing out of the ordinary. If the history of industrialism has
been, in the long term, a history of rising standards of living,
that progress has, until lately, been the result of alternating ups
and downs. It is the abolition of the downs that is the novel
phenomenon.

This is indeed only one aspect of a whole series of paradoxical changes to which economists have had to adapt themselves
in the past twenty years or so. The ups and downs of traditional economic theory used to follow what was at least an

intelligible sequence, although the consequences of this un-wanted rhythm were quite disastrous. First we had booms, during which business ran at full tilt, prices, wages and profits rose and unemployment fell: then the sequence would be reversed and we would have what was called a slump. Prices and wages would fall and the number of unemployed would increase. Now, in place of booms and slumps we have stop – go, and the boom phenomena of rising incomes and prices are inexplicably accompanied by *increased* unemploy-ment.

Nor is this the only, or indeed the most striking, revolution in traditional economic doctrine. In the nineteen-sixties, up to nearly the end of the decade, our economic position was officially said to be indeed parlous. Year after year the balance of payments was in the red, and Britain was repeatedly declared to be teetering on the brink of bankruptcy. Disaster threatened; but nobody ever told us in precise and unmistakable terms just how that disaster would manifest itself should it occur. Should we starve? Would money lose its value in a runaway inflation such as occurred in Germany after the 1914–18 war? Would unemployment reach unprecedented heights? The red figures in the Press and on the TV screens failed to make any serious impact because they were never reflected in the citizen's personal experience. On the contrary, through nearly all this supposedly critical period most people were better off than they had ever been; and, what is even more remarkable, the stock markets soared to an all-time high. Ironically, it was only after it was proclaimed that we were out of the red that rapidly rising inflation caused the man in the street to get seriously alarmed about 'the economy'.

A favourable balance of payments is in fact an extremely difficult objective to sell to the public. Incidentally, it is also (though this never seems to be noticed) a goal at which every country aims, but which it is mathematically impossible for everyone to attain. If we succeed in maintaining our own balance, at whose expense, I wonder, will this be achieved? In Britain, moreover, confusion has been made still more confounded by the fact that the exhortations and advice addressed to us are utterly paradoxical. The only way to escape the nameless terrors said to be lurking round the corner is, we are told, to work harder and produce more. But at the same time, it seems, another necessary though regrettable ingredient in the cure is that the level of unemployment must also rise. In other words, while most people must work harder and produce more, an increasing number of others must be denied the opportunity to work, or to produce anything at all. Science, it is sometimes said, is only organized common sense; but from this dictum, it would seem, contemporary economic science must be excluded.

Deaf to official warnings, therefore, wage and salary earners at every level, along with the business world, have persistently concentrated on improving their personal economic situation; and growing affluence is the measure of their success. But the rewards of this process have been most unequally distributed; or, to put the matter more precisely, they have been distributed in such a way as to make no drastic change in existing inequalities. Poverty has certainly not been eliminated. There are millions still who contribute nothing at all to those rising figures of expenditure on cars and drink and entertainments and holidays abroad. Some millions of our fellow citizens are dependent upon supplementary benefits, and, when their rent is paid, can enjoy (if that is the right word) a weekly income of £5·20 p.w. for a single person, or £8·50 for a married couple (plus an extra 50p for those over pension age and for those under that age who have been on supplementary benefit for at least two years) as from November 1970. Admittedly, these rates are significantly better than what has been paid in the past. But quite apart from the fact that they can hardly be said to represent affluence in any absolute sense, the increase in benefit rates barely keeps pace with the cost of living, and consistently lags behind the general advance in incomes throughout the community as a whole. Moreover, some of the lowest paid will not even get the full rates of supplementary benefit when they are out of work – thanks to the 'wage-stop' rule which does not allow a man's income to be higher when he is unemployed than when he is working.

And there are many such underpaid workers. Two years ago a special enquiry by the Department of Employment and Productivity revealed that one adult male worker in twelve or 900,000 in all were taking home pre-tax earnings of less than £15 per week, while among women workers (whose under-payment is notorious) one in every four or some 200,000 were earning less than £10 a week.[2] Indeed sex differentiation is still so gross that, although the right to equal pay is now on the Statute Book, it has been thought necessary to allow an interval of several years to elapse before it is to be fully operative.

All in all, the contemporary pattern of wages and salaries shows a quite astonishing rigidity. From two distinguished long-term researches we learn, first, that in 1960 the average unskilled male worker's wage was less than one-third of the average manager's salary – which is exactly the ratio that obtained in 1913; and, second, that the relation between the earnings of the top and the bottom 10 per cent of manual

[2] Employment & Productivity Gazette (HMSO, May 1969).

workers is still the same as it was in 1886.[3] During eight years of supposed incomes policy, in spite of brave words in White Papers about the low-paid and about those groups of workers who have been left behind, no intelligible policy ever emerged: respect for the sanctity of differentials is too deeply entrenched. Everybody's income has in fact become fixed by reference to everybody else's. Yet these differentials can claim neither logical nor ethical, neither economic nor social, justification. They are a historical legacy of traditional prestige and of smash-and-grab, masquerading as the divine right of collective bargaining. Fundamentally, they are what they are because they have been what they have been. That is why the matron of a London general hospital never catches up with a mere Principal in the Civil Service, and why a Chief Inspector in the Metropolitan Police at the top of his scale does not get as much as one-twelfth of the salary of the Chairman of the Steel Corporation.

These are gross figures and as such can, as we are often reminded, be misleading. Heavy taxation has certainly modified the shape of the pyramid – but not, in recent years, all that much. In 1959 the top income group to which I referred just now (those with £2,000 or over gross) had an average income *after payment of tax* more than seven times as large as the average post-tax income of the bottom group (that is those with under £600 gross), and nearly three times that of those in the middle section. In 1967 the top class still enjoyed an average post-tax income nearly seven times that of those

---

[3] Quoted in *Poverty*, journal of the Child Poverty Action Group, No. 12/13, 1969, from Routh, G., *Occupation and Pay in Great Britain* 1906–60 (Cambridge University Press, 1965) and Thatcher, A. R., 'The Distribution of Earnings of Employees in Great Britain', *Journal of the Royal Statistical Society*, Series A, Vol., 131, pt. 2, 1968.

remaining at the bottom and nearly two-and-a-half times that of those in the middle; and in 1967 this top group, whose numbers, you may recall, had increased very substantially, were banking (taking home seems an inappropriate expression) an aggregate income of £4,481 million after payment of income and surtax – that is to say 30 per cent more than the £3,397 million shared by more than five times as many people who were still stuck in the bottom class.[4]

I have given some prominence to this aspect of the contemporary picture because its stability reflects, I think, a significant change in the ideology of an important section of political opinion. In the early years of this century, and indeed between the wars, concepts of social equality or social justice held a key position in the philosophy of the Left: they were primary objectives in their own right. Any Labour Government, it was assumed, would not merely eliminate poverty, but would be no less concerned to narrow the gap between the two ends of the income scale. But in the six years of Labour Government that have just ended, while great emphasis has been laid on the importance of increasing the gross national product, considerations of distributive justice appear, incomes policy notwithstanding, to have been relegated to an insignificant position in social policy, if indeed they have not dropped out altogether. I say incomes policy notwithstanding, because that policy has never amounted to more than a (not conspicuously successful) attempt to prevent promiscuous wage and salary increases from inducing a runaway inflation of prices. It has never been directed towards any clear social objective.

Six years, it may be said, is a short time in which to make any radical change in the extremely rigid pattern of British incomes,

[4] Source: Central Statistical Office, National Income and Expenditure (HMSO, 1967 and 1969).

and admittedly the figures which I have quoted relate only to the first four of those six. Later information, when available, might modify the picture; but any dramatic change hardly seems likely. Certainly the readiness with which the late Government conceded salary increases running into thousands for the already highly paid heads of nationalized industries, but boggled over a few pounds here and there for groups of industrial workers, was indisputable evidence that they had completely disassociated themselves from their equalitarian inheritance. The fact that they did so is indeed an eloquent testimony to the strength of what appears to be by far the most dynamic, and the most widespread, motive in our whole social life – that is, the simple desire to get more money. That is why I have added the adjective 'acquisitive' to the more popular terms 'affluent' and 'permissive'.

Collective concentration upon the urgency of increasing the gross national product has almost obliterated concern about who is to enjoy the resulting prosperity, or what may be its price in damage to the natural environment. Individually, the urge to increase one's personal income seems to have obscured any larger vision of the desirable shape of the social pattern. All pretence of an incomes policy having been abandoned in favour of smash-and-grab, it now makes no difference where one stands in the income-scale. Permanent Secretaries in the Civil Service, along with ambassadors and High Commissioners, cast dignity and discretion to the winds to the extent of holding protest meetings, while doctors, offered an immediate 15 per cent rise, restricted their services in the hope of exacting as much again *within a week*. These professions have nothing to learn from striking railwaymen or power workers, or from militant dockers, teachers or nurses. Indeed, acquisitiveness is now widely identified with excellence. In the nationalized industries immensely high salaries at the top are said to be justified as being necessary to attract the best men: undoubtedly they will attract the most acquisitive.

Nevertheless, here and there lone voices in a contrary sense may still be heard. Writing on the eve of the recent General Election on the tasks that would face the incoming Government, Dr A. H. Halsey foretold that 'the distribution, rather than the amount, of national wealth may be the more crucial test' of the Party Manifestos, and concluded that 'not wealth but its distribution will be the mark of whether or not Britain is "great to live in"'.[5] Again, in a study published in 1969 Professor Goldthorpe and others suggested that the right strategy for the Labour Party would be 'a clear commitment to the interests of the mass of wage-earning, rank and file employees, and an endeavour to advance these interests not merely by promoting general economic expansion but also by thorough-going egalitarian measures over a wide front' – even if this should lead to 'strenuous political conflict' and a 'heightening of social antagonisms'.[6] Recently also, the newly elected Swedish Prime Minister, in an interview on British television, claimed that wage policy and taxation in his country were directed towards equality, that increases at top levels were restrained, and that this policy was supported by a 'great movement of opinion'. Could it be that a similar policy in this country might have evoked a comparable movement of opinion, with the result that in the recent Election the outgoing might also have been the incoming Government?

Meanwhile gross inequality of incomes continues to be

[5] Halsey, A. H., 'A Fair Place to Live in?', *New Society*, No. 402, June 11 1970.

[6] Goldthorpe, J. H. *et al*, *The Affluent Worker in the Class Structure* (Cambridge University Press, 1969), p. 193.

accompanied by other not less persistent social inequalities. The hall-mark of a class structure is the division of a community into a recognizable hierarchy of groups between which regular social intercourse (and by consequence inter-marriage) is exceptional, along with a corresponding inequality in access to positions of power and privilege. In contemporary Britain these phenomena are all still conspicuous. Cheerful assertions to the contrary either misinterpret the fact that, with rising standards of living and mass production of clothes, cars and domestic appliances, the various classes look more alike than they did, or mistakenly assume that individual movement between classes involves the disappearance of the classes themselves. Today a miner's son can not only hold exalted political office, but can also rank as a distinguished historian and move in highly cultivated circles in the upper strata of British society, as Roy Jenkins has done; but this does not mean that the men who are still working at the coal face and the members of the intellectual elite normally entertain one another to dinner, still less that they habitually intermarry or have equal opportunities of professional advancement. A rigid class structure is not incompatible with a considerable measure of individual mobility.

Certainly the evidence of social segregation and unequal distribution of power and privilege in contemporary Britain is impressive. Professor Goldthorpe and his colleagues, in the study already mentioned, examined the social life of a sample of manual workers in Luton whose relatively high earnings and good prospects of continued employment suggested that they might be the vanguard of a movement which would obliterate any distinction between the manual and the white-collar classes. Yet it appeared that these workers had remarkably little social contact with their non-manual colleagues: 75 per cent of their most frequent spare-time companions were also manual workers, and two-thirds of them had no white-collar friends at all. At work, moreover, they cherished far less hope of promotion to managerial positions than did their white-collar colleagues – an attitude which is probably realistic, as, with the modern tendency to demand paper qualifications for more and more jobs, it becomes increasingly difficult to elevate oneself from the shop floor merely on the strength of demonstrated competence. This lack of ambition did not, however, extend to these manual workers' hopes for their children: 63 per cent of them wanted their children to have a grammar school education. Yet in only 9 per cent of the sample was this hope realized, whereas, by contrast, a third of the children of office workers in the same establishments found their way to grammar schools.[7]

Differentiation marking the inferior social status of the manual worker is certainly far from obsolete. Recently, Mrs Dorothy Wedderburn has compiled a formidable catalogue of discriminatory practices which work to his disadvantage.[8] Thus the manual worker is likely to get shorter holidays than his office colleagues and less opportunity to choose when to take them. As likely as not, he will be expected to take his meals in a canteen segregated from the clerical and administrative staff; nor can he expect the regular increments on his pay which are normal in administrative or professional employment, the introduction of which, incidentally, might greatly reduce the inflationary effects of pressure for higher wages. If he falls sick, the chances are that, unlike all but a minute proportion of white-collar workers, he will get nothing from his employer to supplement his sickness benefit; and if he has

[7] Ibid., pp. 109, 130, 135.
[8] Wedderburn, Dorothy, 'Inequality at Work', New Society, No. 393, April 9, 1970.

to take time off on account of illness or death in his family, he has much less hope of being paid for it. Finally, when he retires, he is far less likely to receive any addition to his National Insurance pension. All through life in fact he is, even to this day, constantly reminded of his place.

Nor were the Luton workers exceptional in their failure to realize their educational ambitions for their children. A similar picture has emerged from a number of more comprehensive investigations. In his survey of over 5,000 children born in the same week in March 1946 Dr. J. W. B. Douglas found that 54 per cent of those in the upper middle classes, as against 11 per cent of those from the lower manual working classes, achieved a grammar school education; and this differentiation is not to be explained as a reflection of the superior brains of the upper social group. Amongst children with closely similar, but by no means outstanding, scores on intelligence tests, those with upper-middle-class parents were more than twice as likely to be accepted by grammar schools as were those from the ranks of manual workers.[9] Again, a more recent survey of young people who had reached the age of twenty-one in 1962 revealed that 45 per cent of those with fathers in the higher professional class had embarked on full-time higher education, as against only.4 per cent of the sons and daughters of skilled manual workers and a mere 2 per cent of the children of semi- or un-skilled fathers; while the son of a father in any non-manual occupation had nearly four times, and the daughter more than six times, the chance of getting to the top of the educational ladder than had the son or daughter of a man who worked with his hands.[10] Oxford and Cambridge in particular continue to be

[9] Douglas, J. W. B., *The Home and the School* (Macgibbon and Kee, 1964), p. 47.
[10] Committe on Higher Education, *Report* (HMSO, Cmnd 2154, 1963), p. 50.

highly exclusive institutions. According to another survey of University admissions in 1955, 13 per cent of the undergraduates entering Oxford and 9 per cent of those entering Cambridge had manual-working fathers, as against 40 per cent of the entrants to Welsh Universities; and the Robbins Committee, reporting in 1963, concluded that there had probably not been much subsequent change.[11]

Educational exclusiveness is the more important because it bars the road to positions of power and influence. In particular Oxford and Cambridge and the public schools between them are remarkably successful in providing passports both to the higher Civil Service and to judicial office. Of the successful candidates for entry into the Administrative Class of the Civil Service in the years 1948–56, 77 per cent came from Oxford or Cambridge. By 1965, after some fluctuations in both directions, the percentage was still 76.[12] In 1956 39 per cent of the entrants came from public schools, and this figure had actually risen to 43 per cent in the years 1963–7 taken together. 'We know', observed the Public Schools Commission in their Report in 1968, that 'the Civil Service is doing its best to encourage candidates from all universities and from all kinds of school background, and that since 1964 there has been a marked improvement in recruitment from universities other than Oxford and Cambridge'; 'but', the Commissioners modestly added, 'the failure to recruit for the public service from a more representative cross-section of the population is still a matter for concern'.[13]

[11] Committee on Higher Education, *Appendix 2B* (HMSO, Cmnd 2154, 1963), p. 429.

[12] Committee on the Civil Service 1966–8, *Vol. 4, Evidence* (HMSO, 1968), p. 322.

[13] Public Schools Commission, *Report* (HMSO, 1968), pp. 58, 59.

Judicial appointments also are reached by a similar road. A recent investigation by Mr Kevin Goldstein-Jackson has revealed that of the 359 judges, recorders, chairmen of quarter sessions, and stipendiary magistrates whose names appeared in the Law List for 1968, 292, or more than 80 per cent, had been educated at public schools; and at the more exalted levels of the judiciary, all but one of the nine members of the Chancery Division of the High Court came from Oxford or Cambridge and all but one had been to a public school; while of the eighteen judges in the Probate, Admiralty and Divorce Division ten had been to Oxford, six to Cambridge and all but one had either attended public schools or been educated privately.[14]

The persistence of this highly stratified society, with its contrasts of riches and poverty, and its unequal distribution of prestige, privilege and power, is itself the result of one form of permissiveness, that is to say the permissiveness which has renounced any attempt to control the passion for personal enrichment in the interests of any wider vision of a more humane and generous society. Acquisitiveness rampant might well be the most conspicuous feature of our coat of arms. The failure of the feeble attempts of the nineteen-sixties to establish an incomes policy is the more to be regretted, because it has undoubtedly queered the pitch for more promising action in the future.

In the socio-economic sphere this failure faces us, I suspect, with a problem which in the near future may prove even more intractable than that other characteristic menace of our time – our abject reverence for technological ingenuity, culminating in the principle that the more technically difficult an enterprise,

[14] Goldstein-Jackson, Kevin, 'The Judicial Elite', *New Society*, No. 398, May 14, 1970.

the more imperative the necessity of attempting it. On the social damage caused by this subservience to technological insistence I do not propose to expatiate, if only because the subject has suddenly become an extremely popular theme, notably amongst politicians. Cynics may indeed speculate whether it was not fortunate for the late Government that the publication of an entirely admirable White Paper on the Protection of the Environment[15] proved to be one of its dying acts, and that it did not live to reap the discredit of opening a motorway that runs on stilts within twenty feet of people's bedrooms. At least we can say that in regard to the prevention of environmental pollution we have not tried and failed: we have never yet seriously tried, although, if words mean anything, we should be about to do so. But in the war on poverty and on sectional self-seeking, we have at least pretended to try, and the only result has been a catastrophic failure which must inevitably put the clock back.

II

So much for permissiveness in the social and economic sphere. Let us now revert to the more usually accepted meaning of the word, as referring to changes in mental climate in relation to what is regarded as acceptable social behaviour on the one hand, and in the relevant law on the other. Obviously, the two are interconnected, though in a hen-and-egg fashion which it would be difficult to disentangle. The widespread inclusion of sex education in school curricula, and the matter-of-fact readiness of many by no means unconventional contemporary parents to make sure that their teenage daughters are adequately instructed and equipped in the matter of birth control, bear

[15] HMSO, 1970, Cmnd 4373.

striking testimony to the social revolution: such practices would have been unthinkable in similar circles a generation or so earlier. Nevertheless, the extent of these changes in sexual attitudes or behaviour can only be measured by sophisticated investigations; and, although there have been a few such – notably a study by Michael Schofield[16] – any quantitative estimate of the difference between today's and yesterday's opinions and practices is still purely speculative.

Changes in the law, on the other hand, can be precisely stated; and those of the past ten years or so have been pretty dramatic. Within this period we have abolished the Lord Chamberlain's anomalous powers of theatrical censorship, and relaxed the law on obscenity so as to permit the publication, exhibition or stage presentation of anything unless 'its effect . . . is, if taken as a whole, to deprave and corrupt persons' who may read, see or hear it.[17] If, however, the corruption results from a work of literary merit (a question upon which juries have to pronounce) then it escapes the rigour of the law. As a result, we are now permitted to read *Lady Chatterley's Lover* and *Last Exit to Brooklyn*, to look at John Lennon's erotic pictures and to attend performances of *Oh! Calcutta!* At the same time for those who do not share the taste for erotic literature or for nude theatrical spectacles, or whose appetites for these indulgences may have been sated, other opportunities for recreation have been opened by the relaxation of the betting and gambling laws. The betting shop is now a normal feature of every High Street and the one-armed bandit a ubiquitous temptation, while an Act of 1960 opened the door to bingo and other forms of gambling – although in the light of later

---

[16] Schofield, Michael, *The Sexual Behaviour of Young People* (Longmans, 1965).
[17] Obscene Publications Act, 1959.

experience, the last-named pastimes have subsequently been subjected to geographical and other restrictions, such that devotees of these pursuits would do well to choose their place of residence carefully.

Meanwhile a rapid succession of Acts of Parliament has enlarged our freedom in sexual matters. In 1967 male homosexuality was legalized for consenting adults (other than members of the Armed Forces) in private, subject to the restriction that the crews of merchant ships must not engage in homosexual practices on a UK vessel, whether at sea or in port. In the same year feminine freedoms also were enlarged by the Abortion Act, which allows a pregnancy to be terminated if its continuance would involve a risk to the life of the pregnant woman or of injury to her mental or physical health, or to that of her existing children, greater than that which would be involved in its termination. In addition, termination is legalized if there is a substantial risk that the child will be born with a serious mental or physical handicap. Women have certainly not been slow to avail themselves of these facilities. In 1969 more than 54,000 prospective mothers managed to convince two doctors that their cases complied with one or other of those conditions, 33,000 of them occupying National Health Service beds for their operations.[18]

Two years later Parliament passed the Divorce Reform Act, which makes the irretrievable breakdown of a marriage the sole ground for divorce. This Act has been described as simultaneously legalizing divorce by consent and divorce without consent, since one of the conditions which may constitute proof of breakdown is that the parties, having lived apart for the two years immediately preceding, both consent to the dissolution of the marriage; while, alternatively, a marriage may be

[18] House of Lords *Hansard*, written answer, March 3, 1970.

dissolved on the petition of one spouse, without the consent of the other, after five years' such separation.

Most of these measures other than the new divorce law have one feature in common – namely, that they sanction types of behaviour which involve no injury to third parties. If I disapprove of gambling, I can keep away from bingo halls and fruit machines. If I do not want to read *Last Exit to Brooklyn* or to see *Oh! Calcutta!* I am under no compulsion to do so. I may be shocked that other people have different tastes and, in the supposed interests of their morals, may deplore the fact that they should be permitted to gratify these. But I do not thereby suffer a personal injury such as is inflicted on the victim of a burglary or assault. Recent 'permissive' legislation deals, in fact, with 'victimless' actions, the only exceptions being the case in which a divorce is forced upon an unwilling spouse without his or her consent, and the foetus who is destroyed by an abortion. With these exceptions, the new laws legitimize actions which have hitherto been prohibited, not because of the injury that they cause to others, but because they are held to be in some sense 'wrong in themselves'.

Many of these Acts, moreover, originated in Private Members' Bills for which governments formally disclaimed responsibility, although in some cases their sponsors received so much official help, by way of drafting or allocation of Parliamentary time, that the pretence of governmental neutrality wore rather thin. At every stage, however, MPs were left free to vote, as the saying goes, 'according to their consciences', and without directions from the Whips (a formula which incidentally seems to carry the curious implication that on all Government business either no issue of conscience can arise, or its promptings must be ignored). The passage of these laws may thus be read as evidence that the consciences of members of

Parliament, or at least members' interpretations of the public conscience, are on the move.

Here, I think, we touch upon one of the most significant social trends of the time. It would seem that in effect we now live in a society whose moral codes are derived from two alternative sources; and that one of these is demonstrably gaining upon the other. The first embodies traditional religious precepts and relies upon religious sanctions. This code labels certain actions as inherently sinful. In the debates in the Lords on the Sexual Offences Bill of 1967 the Anglican Bishops made it perfectly clear that, even if they supported a change in the law, they nevertheless regarded homosexual practices as inherently immoral. In the Commons' discussion of the Divorce Reform Bill one MP boldly asserted that 'in Christian marriage there are not two parties to the contract: there are three – the husband, the wife and Almighty God.'[19] Again, to Mr George Thomas, Secretary of State for Wales in the late Labour Government, gambling was 'a sin', and its legalization was to be condemned as 'against those who are seeking to build a Christian order of society';[20] and to Catholics abortion is abhorrent even in some instances to the point of preferring the life of the foetus to that of the mother.

Such judgements are necessarily absolute and authoritarian inasmuch as they claim to express the will of God or to embody the teaching of the Christian Church. They are, therefore, acceptable only to those who believe in God, recognize the authority of the Church, and agree that by these precepts his will is correctly interpreted. For the agnostic they can have no validity; and discussion of them between agnostic and Christian can only be sterile, since it cannot go beyond the point at

[19] House of Commons *Hansard*, June 12, 1969, Col. 2036.
[20] House of Commons *Hansard*, November 16, 1959, Col. 848.

which one party says 'I believe this' and the other replies 'I don't'. The agnostic or humanist, on the other hand, recognizes an alternative secular morality which claims no supernatural authority. For him the question of the morality or immorality of any action is simply a matter of its social effect. Actions which in any way damage someone else are immoral; and this is the only relevant criterion.

Fortunately for the smooth working of our society, the practical implications of these two moral systems overlap extensively. Christians, being exhorted to love their neighbours as themselves, generally regard behaviour which is injurious to others as iniquitous. But, as already indicated, they also condemn certain types of conduct as sinful, irrespective of its consequences; and on occasions, as when they hold a divorce to be immoral even in circumstances in which it is desired by all the parties concerned, these moral absolutes over-ride any considerations of what would make for the greatest happiness of the greatest number: marriage, as a sacred institution, and God as the third party to Christian marriage, must take precedence over husband, wife and children too. Hence at this point the two moral systems part company. Occasionally, the consequential practical conflict may be mitigated by the willingness of some Christians to concede that on some issues what may be called the higher, non-social, morality should be a matter only for the individual conscience, and need not be written into the law. It was, as I have mentioned, on these grounds that some dignitaries of the Church were able to reconcile themselves to the legalization of adult homosexual practices. But similar concessions are not made by the Catholics in relation to divorce, nor by many Christians in relation to the relaxation of censorship, or to gambling or abortion.

I said just now that of the two contemporary systems or

morality one seems to be gaining on the other – and I meant, of course, that the permissive legislation of the past few years reflects the erosion of religious belief in our community, and the substitution, in its place, of a purely secular social morality, which recognizes no absolutes and no supernatural sanctions, and for which the wicked action is the one that injures, and the virtuous action the one that benefits, others. This, it would seem, is the judgement of the collective conscience that led Parliament to pass the legislation that I have described.

Have we then reached the end of the road? I see no reason to suppose so. Some bastions still survive, but are likely to prove increasingly vulnerable. Two recent attempts to legalize euthanasia have met with early deaths in Parliament. But it is now nine years since suicide, actual or attempted, ceased to be a crime, though it is still an offence to aid, abet, counsel or procure the suicide of another. If, then, it is permissible to kill oneself, would it not be logical to allow a right, in the event of personal incapacity, to entrust the task to someone else? Again, Parliament has repeatedly refused to abolish the regulations that still restrict Sunday entertainments; yet in a secular community are not these prohibitions bound eventually to be regarded as anomalous? Controversy about the continuance of compulsory religious education in schools is also spreading more widely. Not so long ago opposition to this compulsion hardly extended beyond the ranks of confessed humanists. Now doubts have crept into some of the teachers' organizations. In April 1970 the National Association of Schoolmasters proposed that the statutory requirements for religious education and religious worship should be rescinded, on the ground that it is unrealistic to hope that compulsory religious worship and instruction will have the effects which its advocates desire.[21] Meanwhile from within the bosom of the Established Church itself, the Report of the Bishop of Durham's Committee has made some tentative and timid proposals for liberalization.[21] Subsequently, in a television interview the Bishop summarized his Committee's recommendations as a proposal to put religious education on the same footing in the school curriculum as mathematics; though how far this is compatible with some crucial passages in the Committee's Report is a matter on which I shall throw some doubt in my final lecture.

Compulsory religious education is certainly vulnerable. And so, I think, are the last relics of censorship. So much has already passed the barriers that it is likely to become increasingly difficult to justify their retention, the more so as some of the most civilized nations in Europe have already abolished censorship altogether.

What then is the end of the road? Recently this has been well described by two distinguished criminologists, writing in Chicago,[23] who, in all seriousness, suggest the total abolition of all 'victimless' offences. Spelled out in American terms, this would mean the removal from the criminal calendar of everything to do with drunkenness, misuse of drugs, gambling, sexual behaviour (including incest and bestiality), abortion and 'disorderly conduct and vagrancy' – the only exceptions being cases involving juveniles. Undoubtedly some of the items in this list are improbable candidates for legalization in this country (and in the United States also, one would imagine). Legislation about the misuse of drugs, in particular, is the one

---

[21] *The Times*, April 24, 1970.

[22] *The fourth R: Report of the Commission on Religious Education in Schools* (SPCK, 1970).

[23] Morris, Norval and Hawkins, Gordon, *The Honest Politician's Guide to Crime Control* (University of Chicago Press, 1970).

outstanding exception to the generally permissive trend of recent years. Although the Bill which the present Government has taken over from its predecessors reduces the penalties for illegal possession of certain drugs, notably cannabis, it raises the maximum sentence for illicit supply from ten years' imprisonment to fourteen, with the possibility of an unlimited fine in addition; and these penalties, moreover, may await the doctor who defies a Home Secretary's order to cease over-prescribing a particular drug. But even in relation to drugs, a not inconsiderable body of opinion holds that the ban on cannabis is not worth the cost of its enforcement, and, in some cases, that mere possession of any drug ought not to be criminal.

However much further we may travel along the permissive road, there can be little doubt as to the speed with which the secularization of the community is proceeding. The decline in religious observance is both visible to the naked eye and well-attested statistically. As the Rev. Kenneth Slack observed in the Introduction to the second edition of his book on *The British Churches Today* 'The revision of the statistics alone has all too fully confirmed the personal impression gained of the accelerating decline of the Church as an institution throughout the period . . . It is still possible to write of the British Churches today in the light of history: shortly the operation may assume more the character of archaeology burrowing beneath a collapsed edifice.' The Church of England in particular is threatened by a 'staggering drop' of nearly 59 per cent in five years in the number of recommended candidates for ordination. 'In almost all the Churches,' comments Mr Slack, 'theological colleges have been falling like the leaves in autumn.' In the ten years to 1966 the ratio of baptisms to population dropped by 15 per cent (the decline in the metropolitan area being more than twice as fast), and in six years the ratio of confirmations to population fell by almost one-third. Nor have the Nonconformist churches fared any better. According to Mr Slack's figures membership of the Baptist Churches has fallen from nearly 434,700 in 1906 to 285,000 in 1967; while the number of children attending Baptist Sunday schools fell from 590,000 in 1906 to 310,700 in 1957 and to 228,000 in 1967. The Congregationalists' 456,600 members in 1909 had sunk to less than 180,000 sixty years later; and these losses have all to be measured against a steeply rising population.[24] Only the Catholics claim a rising membership in recent years, and this is unquestionably affected by Irish immigration into this country. Summarizing the whole situation in a book published in 1966, Bryan Wilson concluded that 'at the very highest estimate . . . fewer than 25 per cent of the adult population of England & Wales has any real claim to be "in membership" of any religious denomination'; while average church attendance on Sunday was estimated at not more than 10 per cent to 15 per cent of the population.[25] Since then a later survey by the Independent Television Authority has found that half the British population (outside N. Ireland) either disbelieve in God altogether or have no certain conviction of his existence; and that more than half say that religious belief has not very much effect, or none at all, upon their everyday lives.[26]

This decline in the influence of religion undoubtedly represents one of the most significant social changes between this century and its immediate predecessor. Reading, for example,

[24] Slack, Kenneth, *The British Churches Today* (SCM Press, 1970), pp. xi, xiii, 54.
[25] Wilson, Bryan *Religion in Secular Society* (Penguin Books, 1969), pp. 22, 25.
[26] *Religion in Britain & Northern Ireland: A Survey of Popular Attitudes* (Independent Television Authority, 1970), pp. 19, 28.

E. M. Forster's delightful life of his great-aunt Marianne Thornton, one cannot but be struck by the unquestioning acceptance by educated people right up to the last decades of the nineteenth century of the literal truth of the traditional Christian doctrines, and by their absolute certainty that every bereavement would in due course be followed by a happy reunion. Even now I question whether we fully appreciate the difference that the loss of this faith has made to our outlook on life; and I shall have more to say in my final lecture both on the reaction of the churches themselves to their vanishing influence and on the social consequences of secularization. But in the present context the significant implication of this trend is that it undermines the basis of the moral judgements which condemn certain forms of behaviour as reprehensible in themselves, irrespective of their social consequences. The critic who reviles homosexuality, or nudity on the stage, or the proliferation of betting shops and bingo clubs must now shift his ground from categorical denunciation of sin, to face the question 'What harm do they do?' On these issues, in short, a secular, socially-based standard of morality is gradually establishing itself. But regrettably, by contrast, in relation to personal economic greed, no standard at all, not even hatred of Mammon, has yet placed any restraint on total permissiveness.

2

THE DEMOCRATIC PROCESS

The democratic process appears to be in the doldrums. Demonstrations and riots testify to widespread frustration and to a growing conviction that traditional democratic procedures are hopelessly ineffectual instruments for making government bend to the demands of the people. For most of us democracy means no more than the right to choose between alternative governments at four- or five-year intervals without recourse to force. Even on these occasions, moreover, the task of making rational choices is almost impossibly difficult. The Government of the day can indeed present its record which we may or may not like; but the door is wide open for its rivals to indulge in flights of fantasy which are not easily evaluated. In this respect Mr Heath's opening broadcast in the 1970 election, with its promises that his Government would control inflation at one stroke without a prices and incomes policy, legislate against strikes, reduce Government expenditure, cut taxes and maintain British forces in the Far East must have set something of a record. In view of what has happened since, one is almost tempted to wonder whether he was banking upon not being victorious. But no matter which party wins, for the succeeding four or five years, it seems, They can do what they like with Us.

The contemporary mood of disillusion is, I think, due to two changes occurring on two different levels. First, the past century has seen revolutionary modifications of our domestic political conventions with which we do not seem yet fully to have come to terms; and second, world-wide technological developments have everywhere increasingly complicated the business of government and the mutual relations of government and governed.

On the domestic scene, the primary problem is that the Parliamentary system has lost its historical function and failed to find a satisfactory substitute. To a politically powerless Monarchy, a near-functionless Upper Chamber (which, in the classic words of Iolanthe, does nothing in particular and does it very well) we are now in danger of adding a robot House of Commons. Parliament was evolved as an organ of government in which issues of public concern were debated, and decisions made by the members in the light of those discussions. But as everybody knows, it is now nothing of the kind. Or, even now, does everybody know? As recently as the nineteen-fifties, schools were apparently still perpetuating the myth of Parliamentary supremacy. In an examination for university entrance at that time I once asked candidates how, if they were members of Parliament, they would expect to spend their time and what they would regard as their most important duties. Almost without exception they drew pictures of the open-minded MP, conscientiously listening with rapt attention to debates in the House, and, in the light of what he heard there, casting his vote in what he judged to be the best interests of the nation in general and his constituents in particular. Not one of them, to the best of my recollection, appeared to have heard of political parties or Whips; and yet as potential university students they might be expected to be more than averagely intelligent and well-informed.

Only in marginal cases is Parliament now a decision-making body. The recent 'permissive' legislation discussed in my first lecture occupied only a negligible fraction of Parliamentary time by comparison with the steady flow of Government Bills which are dutifully enacted by the votes of the majority Party. In the life of the 1966–70 Parliament opposition in the House of Commons did indeed compel the Government to drop their Bill to reform the House of Lords; and the threat of opposition forced them to abandon their plans for radical legislation on the subject of strikes; but that is about the total score. True, the House of Commons can and does amend Government Bills, but only in so far as members can make their proposals acceptable to Ministers. As for the legislative powers of the Lords in relation to Government Bills, these hardly amount to more than a ritual dance (which, considering the archaic constitution of the so-called Upper House, is doubtless something to be thankful for). Much time is spent by their Lordships in discussion of amendments to Government Bills; but any of these which are passed against the wishes of the Government will be rejected by the Commons – after which their Lordships will invariably give in gracefully but ungrammatically, by passing the motion 'That this House doth not insist on its Amendments to which the Commons have disagreed'.

This decline in the power and prestige of Parliament not only breeds disillusioned MPs, but also has inevitable repercussions upon the general public. Old-fashioned methods of voicing popular opinion, such as writing letters to one's Member, or bombarding him with resolutions passed by innumerable societies begin to look somewhat futile. At best he may say a few brave words in the House or behind the scenes; but the chances of influencing his vote, in any but exceptional cases, are negligible. One has a far better chance of success by organizing a public demonstration or getting somebody to put one's case on the telly.

In part, as I have suggested, these problems are indigenous to this country. An American Congressman has much more freedom then a British MP to vote as he thinks fit, not as he is told. Nevertheless, the world over, the democratic process as we have known it is more fundamentally threatened by three significant trends. The first is the drive towards centralization and the clash of local initiative with the demand for uniformity; the second arises from the irreconcilable conflicts of interest in an increasingly differentiated society; and the third, from the growing complexity of the issues involved in the business of government and the invention of new methods of decision-making.

Of these problems the first is well illustrated by the recent history of public education. Wherever selective secondary education is the rule, a child's chance of getting to a grammar school depends, not merely on his ability, but also on the resources of the area in which he happens to live. If grammar-school places are provided on a relatively generous scale, they will be open to children who, in a poorer area, would be excluded. This seems both absurd and unjust. It might be less objectionable in an era of lower mobility when one county was pretty well segregated from another and even unaware of what its neighbour was doing; but it makes no sense in our tight little island. And this is only one example from one service, which could be multiplied many hundred times from the differing policies of local authorities in, say, housing, child-care or local health services. The dilemma is always this – that the larger the unit, the more inaccessible it necessarily becomes to the ordinary citizen, and the more the Them-and-Us situation is likely to develop. Yet centralization is the inevitable price of eliminating anomalies and injustices as between the residents in one area and another. Hence the practical question: at what point does a local system of education (or child-care or housing policy) become as ridiculous as it would have been to retain different gauge railways in different parts of the country?

The second threat to the democratic process in contemporary society, namely the irreconcilability of conflicting interests, hardly needs illustration. The motorist wants new, fast roads. People whose houses are pulled down in order to make these roads, or who are faced with an elevated motorway running just outside and level with their bedroom windows, are understandably furious. Nearly everybody apparently wants the hostel for drug addicts, the prison or the new airport to go somewhere outside his own neighbourhood; and so on. Nor must it be assumed that these are always conflicts between different people. Sometimes, though generally unrecognized as such, they are conflicts within one and the same person. About that I shall have more to say presently.

The growing complexity of the process of decision-making is also obvious enough, alike to those who do, and to those who do not, have to take part in it. In the past few years governments have had to decide whether or not to introduce an incomes policy, and in the former case, what sort of policy this should be, and how it should be made effective. In either case decisions have had to be taken about the pay of the Civil Servants who are the Government's own employees, as also about that of doctors, teachers, nurses. Agricultural prices for the coming year have to be discussed with farmers, and then settled, with, or more probably without, their agreement. Existing legislation about the misuse of drugs having obviously failed to keep pace with the realities of the ever-changing drug scene, a new Bill must be drafted; while the need for comprehensive reorganization of British seaports, or of our aircraft industry must be examined; and eventually, of course, some unfortunate government will have to decide when (if ever) and where to build a new international airport. And so on.

Such decisions, moreover, generally have indirect repercussions that extend far beyond the immediate issues involved. Thus, legislation about misuse of drugs affects not only drug addicts themselves, but manufacturers and pharmacists, and doctors who may be faced with restrictions upon their cherished freedom to prescribe as in their wisdom they think fit. Obviously also every decision about a wage or salary claim must be considered in the light of its effect upon differentials and upon possible claimants in other occupations; and it is hardly necessary to emphasize the endless repercussions of decisions about the siting of an airport upon local amenities, upon the destruction of agricultural land, upon the ejection of people from their homes, and upon employment prospects. The Roskill Commissioners have digested some three million words on these and related topics, and now that they have finished, the Government still has to decide whether or not their recommendation is right.

II

How then does the democratic process cope with these conditions? How far has it kept pace with the times? In recent years the traditional right to vote has certainly been supplemented by several devices designed to make the voice of the people heard. The polls and surveys, for example, which are now such a familiar feature of the social and political landscape, are one of the most significant inventions of the past half-century. It was not, I think, until the first world war that the late Professor Bowley pioneered the use of sampling methods in an investigation into social conditions in the potteries – at a time when the now renowned Dr Gallup was still a student. Now, as everybody knows, the sample survey is extensively used in market research, in ascertaining public reaction to all manner of issues, from capital punishment to daylight saving, or from the hours at which shops should close to the influence of television upon criminal behaviour; and, of course, in fore-casting the results of elections. Governments no longer have any excuse for not knowing what the public thinks. They can always ask, and if they don't ask, we can initiate our own polls and tell them.

And, undoubtedly, they do sometimes take notice. It can hardly have been coincidental that the Labour Government's decision to re-introduce prescription charges, followed upon a poll which showed widespread public readiness to accept this change; and it is significant that in 1966 the Department of Economic Affairs immediately asked for full particulars of a survey which had indicated certain conditions in which majority opinion would accept a wage freeze; and that not long afterwards, in contravention of its election manifesto, the Government proceeded to impose such a freeze. That is not, of course, to say that governments on all occasions slavishly follow the dictates of the polls. Sometimes they think that they know best, as the present Government does in relation to the Common Market, and as a Parliamentary majority did in rela-tion to hanging; but when they do ignore the pollsters' findings, they are apt to be abused by their opponents. Obviously also any Prime Minister will take account of the polls in deciding when to dissolve Parliament. Mr Wilson did indeed tell us that he had privately settled on a June election quite early in 1970, before the forecasts moved so dramatically in Labour's favour; but does anyone believe that he would have stuck to his opinion if they had continued to predict a substantial Tory majority?

All this, of course, assumes that opinion polls, and in particular election forecasts, are generally valid; whereas the pollsters, like the democratic process itself, are today widely supposed to be in the doldrums – totally unreliable guides in whom we should no longer place any credence. Yet this scepticism, based as it is merely on mistaken predictions as to the result of the 1970 election, is, in fact, remarkably superficial. An election forecast can go wrong for a number of reasons: people may change their minds between the date on which it is recorded and the actual election; there may be a large number who refuse to commit themselves or give misleading answers; the poll may be technically at fault in relying on an inadequate or biased sample; or the investigators may be careless, slovenly or plain dishonest. On this last point one investigator who has taken part in a number of surveys has recently published an account of his own experiences. In one case he records that he and his colleagues were employed to get the reactions of local people to a council housing project. Many tenants, however, fearing that this might be the prelude to a rent increase, refused to answer questions or 'told a series of patent lies'. Others were Greek and could not speak English. So the investigators took their money and reported 'the number we first thought of and hoped for the best'. Again, when employed on a by-election forecast, the author of these confessions and his colleagues 'never stirred from the pub that stands near the Labour Party Committee rooms'. One is glad to learn that he has 'given up polling now'.[1]

All these things *can* happen. But many are, at least, up to a point, avoidable. Carelessness and dishonesty can be minimized by various devices for detection and supervision, and to this matter the experts have given much attention. The cheat certainly cannot be confident of getting away with it. Other factors admittedly introduce an inevitable element of uncertainty into what, after all, cannot be more than an estimate of probabilities. But the facts hardly justify the sweeping assertion of the author just quoted that 'A major reason that the polls have hitherto enjoyed such a reputation is that their findings are mostly irrefutable.' The one type of poll the findings of which are subject to validation is the election forecast; and the record here in this country is remarkably good. The Gallup organization, which was the first to be established here and which alone has covered every general election since the second world war, correctly forecast the result of seven out of the eight post-war elections, their one failure being the election of 1970. In these seven elections the average difference between Gallup estimates of the votes to be won by each Party and those actually recorded was 1·1 per cent, the maximum error being 2·9 per cent. Furthermore, since 1960 Gallup have covered twenty British by-elections, getting the right result in eighteen of these. In these twenty elections the average error in estimating any one party's share of the votes has been 2·7 per cent. This figure, however, is inflated by the two cases in which the forecast was wrong: if these are eliminated, the average error drops to under 2 per cent. Over the world as a whole Gallup Poll Institutes claim to have covered more than 800 elections and to have failed to predict the correct result in less

[1] Williams, Max, 'Up the Polls', *New Society*, No. 406, 9 July 1970.

than twenty of these: thus the odds are forty to one against a Gallup forecast being wrong.[2] It is, therefore, quite absurd to dismiss all polls as invalid on the strength of one recent failure.

Some years ago it was even – perhaps somewhat light-heartedly – suggested by Dr Maurice Kendall that a properly conducted sample poll would actually give a better representation of the public's political preferences than does the present system of election by universal access to the ballot-box: in other words a sample poll might be a more democratic method of electing a government than is a General Election. If actual votes, not merely voting intentions, were recorded, there would of course be no question of errors in forecasting such as now arise from respondents' subsequent changes of mind, or from vague or misleading answers: the sample would vote by secret ballot as in an election. In that case, on the assumption that the sample was large enough and accurately mirrored the various sub-groups in the population, this method could claim superiority over the universal ballot, inasmuch as it would not be distorted by the inability of electors who were ill or absent from home to get to the polling station. A truly representative sample could thus give a more accurate representation of opinion than a nominally universal survey which is biased by accidental omissions.

No one of course seriously suggests that the introduction of such a system would be a practical proposition. Technical perfection in sampling methods is not attainable, and, even if it were, for the public to accept a sample instead of a theoretically universal popular vote would indeed demand a high degree of

[2] The Gallup Election Handbook (The Gallup Poll, June 1970) and personal communication from Mr Geoffrey Faulder, Research Director, The Gallup Poll, to whom I am much indebted.

statistical sophistication. Even in relation to existing polls, how often does one not hear the would-be derogatory comment that 'no one has ever interviewed me'! Nevertheless the theoretical basis of Dr Kendall's proposal is unchallengeable; and anyone who observed the remarkable accuracy with which the BBC's computer foretold the outcome of the 1970 general election on the results of only a handful of constituencies can hardly fail to be impressed by the potentialities of modern methods of statistical prediction. Certainly the performance of the sample survey in the one field in which its accuracy can be tested is sufficiently impressive to justify a high degree of confidence in its findings in other contexts. Indisputably it has enormously improved the quality of communication between people and government.

This at least provides one safeguard against the pressure towards centralization in government which I have listed as the first of the three fundamental threats to the democratic process in the modern world. Small local authorities must surrender their powers to larger ones, and more and more decisions must be made by the central Government and not at any local level. But the larger an authority's area, the more remote its members from their constituents. One can perhaps make a real impact upon the parish council, one may be on dining-and-wining terms with one's representative on the district or borough council, but the county council is veiled in a misty distance, and the larger authorities proposed by the Redcliffe-Maud Commission, or whatever the present Government may substitute for them, will be mistier still. In so far as modern survey techniques have made it easier to peer through the mists so that They can see what We want, and how We react to what They are doing, we have indeed cause to be grateful. Even if these techniques do not of themselves wholly resolve the dilemma of centralization versus popular control, we should undoubtedly be much worse off without them.

III

Communication, however, communicates conflict as often as common objectives. Many of these conflicts, let us face it, cannot be wholly resolved. How odd to think that, even within this century, academically respectable authors were solemnly writing about the General Will, reducing the function of government to the simple task of ascertaining the content of that Will and giving it legislative effect! In the realities of contemporary life, too often the best that can be hoped for is some sort of compromise between a vast network of highly specialized wills.

In one sphere at least, that of physical planning, this country can claim to have made a determined effort to resolve such conflicts by democratic procedures. I myself can never attend a local planning enquiry without deeply regretting that there are no observers present from behind the Iron Curtain. The procedure may be slow and tedious and unnecessarily protracted by the ingenuity of the legal profession, while great inconvenience is also caused by the long queue of cases awaiting the Minister's decision. But those of us who are old enough to remember what happened when nothing of the kind existed cannot but recognize that British planning legislation is a remarkable experiment in adapting the democratic process to the contentious issues almost invariably raised whenever anybody wants to build a house or even to put up a garage where no garage was before.

Recently further developments of public participation (to use a fashionable word) have been proposed by a Departmental

Committee presided over by Mr Arthur Skeffington,[3] during his term of office as one of the Parliamentary Secretaries to the then Ministry of Housing and Local Government. Public participation, this Committee suggested, should be invited 'at the formative stage in the making of development plans'. Questions to be discussed might include 'Should a city be substantially expanded? If so in what form? Should development in the vicinity of a historic town be substantially curbed in order to conserve its character or is there scope for establishing a new centre?' Public participation in deciding these issues was to be sought, first, by an announcement that a structure plan is to be prepared; next, by surveys of facts and opinions; then by 'identification, on a broad scale, of the possibilities and choices open to the community'; and finally by submission of 'favoured proposals' for public discussion. The members of the Skeffington Committee were certainly most assiduous in their efforts to make this consultation real. Not only did they urge the establishment of community forums representative of organizations active in the area of each planning authority; they were no less concerned to seek out the views of those who do not join societies or attend meetings. This they thought might be achieved by the appointment of community development officers who would move around the district making casual contacts with individuals (in the pub perhaps, or the laundrette?) in order to glean the views of the inarticulate.

Mr Skeffington and his colleagues were equally determined that no one should have any excuse for complaining that he did not know what his local authority was up to in its development plans. Their Report has, however, been criticized – notably by

[3] *People and Planning*, Report of the Committee on Participation in Planning (HMSO, 1969).

Mr Derek Senior[4] – on the ground that it should have gone even further. If a local authority indicates its own preference between possible alternatives, the critics fear that the public will refuse to believe that the options are genuinely open. Not only, they say, should no such preferences be revealed: the authority should invite public discussion before it has actually made up its own mind about which plan it likes best. Such an extension of public participation was, however, unacceptable to Mr Skeffington and his colleagues on the ground that it would be 'confusing'. Nevertheless the criticism has force, and it seems to have been taken to heart, notably by the South Hampshire Plan Advisory Committee, representing the Hampshire County Council and the Portsmouth and Southampton City Councils. This Committee, without committing itself to any one of them, has publicized and invited public comment upon four main possibilities for the development of the area covered by these three authorities and for the provision of accommdation for its rapidly growing population.

Failure thus to offer choice between alternatives has indeed bedevilled all our planning procedures. Here there are lessons to be learned from the Stansted affair. The choice of a site for a new airport never could have been just Stansted or nothing: when the Government originally decided on Stansted they were not making a real choice at all, since they had no alternatives between which to choose. So also in the numerous and highly controversial proposals for sites for new reservoirs, which are constantly being submitted for ministerial approval, no alternatives are normally presented: the Minister's task is merely to say yea or nay to a particular proposal. Inasmuch as it re-

[4] Senior, Derek, 'Public Involvement in Planning', *The Future of the Social Services* (ed. Robson, W. H. and Crick, Bernard, Pelican Books, 1970).

quires decisions to be reached on only a fraction of the relevant evidence, this procedure may fairly be criticized as wasteful, inept and unjudicial.

Local planning decisions are bound to place great strains upon the democratic process on account of the acute conflicts of interest which they habitually involve. Can any improvements in the process be devised to meet this situation? Professor David Donnison thinks that they can. Being suspicious that the Skeffington 'forums' might prove to be merely talking shops, he would prefer to rely on sampling techniques which would produce regular community surveys. Under his plan, a panel of say 5,000 people would be chosen by random selection in a given local authority area. This panel would then be regularly questioned on a variety of topics and their answers published. The panel 'might want to know how many mothers want a day nursery for their children, how many old people seek rate rebates or know they may be entitled to them, and how many of those who get their "first choice" of secondary schools are genuinely satisfied with that choice?' All of these, Professor Donnison sagely observes, are questions the answers to which the authorities might like to omit or suppress. To the criticism that random selection might result in the inclusion in the panel of some crazy eccentrics, Donnison replies that eccentrics have as much right to be heard as anybody else; and anyhow, if membership of the panel was limited in duration, any impossible people would be got rid of in due course.[5]

The Donnison proposal, which its author thinks might be tried out experimentally in a new or expanding town, certainly has its attractions; though one can see that the great majority of

[5] Donnison, David, 'Government and Governed', *New Society*, No. 388, March 5, 1970.

citizens who would not be members of the panel might be furiously resentful of the apparent privilege conferred on those who were.

In addition to these relatively newfangled devices, that ancient and extreme form of democratic mechanism – the referendum – has recently shown some signs of creeping back into favour. It has, for instance, been suggested that so drastic a constitutional change as entry into the Common Market ought not to be made unless we have all had an opportunity of expressing our approval or disapproval of it; and there were those who urged that the proposal to abolish the death penalty ought likewise to have been subject to a referendum. In support of the former case parallels can be quoted from our own attitude to proposed constitutional change in our former dependencies or other Commonwealth territories. It was, we insisted, for the Gibraltarians themselves to say whether they wanted to join with Spain or remain British. On the question of the death penalty, on the other hand, it was the moral quality of the issue which, it was suggested, made decision by referendum appropriate.

For my part I do not think that either of these is a good case for a referendum. The decision to join or not to join the Common Market involves considerations of fantastic complexity. Even the late Government's White Paper[6] on the subject was (and was apparently intended to be) a masterpiece of ambiguity; and certainly the vast majority of the electorate are in no position to give a sensible judgement about it. As for the abolition of capital punishment, this is undoubtedly a moral issue. But more than morality is involved. The argument most commonly used in support of the death penalty relies on

[6] *Britain and The European Communities: An Economic Assessment* (HMSO, 1970, Cmnd 4289).

its supposedly unique force as a deterrent. The validity of this argument can, however, only be tested by observation of empirical evidence from areas in which capital punishment is or is not in force; and members of the general public are unlikely to have access to that evidence or to be able to assess its weight if they had – especially since it has generally been ignored by supporters of the death penalty.

This, however, is not to deny that some questions, even in the complex contemporary world, might appropriately be decided by referendum. One possible example might have been the question of retaining British Standard Time. This is a matter that affects everybody personally. Some people like the present arrangement and some do not; nor, as far as I can see, are there any other complicating factors to be taken into account. So it might well have been settled by the simple process of counting the likes and the dislikes and letting the majority view prevail. A free vote in Parliament may have been the next best thing, but what a boost it would have been to democratic morale to have been allowed actually to make this ourselves!

Merely counting heads, however, is not always enough. Heads sometimes need to be evaluated as well as counted, particularly for the intensity of their concern in any given controversy. To take an obvious example, there are doubtless thousands of motorists who would welcome a new motorway providing a quick exit from London to the West. But these views cannot be weighed on a one-for-one basis against the distress of people who are suddenly faced with a road on stilts (have we learned nothing from the old New York El?) and continuous traffic roaring past their bedroom windows. Whether or not this is one of them, there are clearly cases where a minority interest ought to prevail.

Unfortunately, however, there is no easy method of evaluating the rival claim in such conflicts. For all the current talk about cost-benefits analysis, quantifying the unquantifiable remains an arbitrary process that can give no mathematically defensible results. As such it can sometimes be useful (e.g. in points systems for the allocation of houses) in ensuring consistency of judgement; but it can give no security that these judgements are consistently right rather than consistently wrong.

This, perhaps, is where demonstrations have a part to play. A demonstration is no use as a guide to the numerical extent of any opinion. It can always be discounted by reference to what President Nixon likes to call the 'silent majority'. But it is a rough index of the intensity of feeling on controversial issues or sectional grievances. People only demonstrate on matters about which they care deeply. One might even suggest paradoxically that, for this reason, self-interested demonstrations deserve more attention than those which deal with general questions. On issues such as the war in Vietnam or the South African cricket tour, in which most of the people of this country have no direct personal involvement, it is arguable that no one's opinion deserves to carry extra weight, merely because he shouts louder than his fellows, and that counting heads is the right democratic procedure; whereas the Westway demonstrators had a peculiar personal interest, not shared by the rest of the community, which entitled them to special consideration. This argument is perhaps not without merit, though I do not myself find it conclusive.

IV

Sample surveys, community forums, new methods of public participation, demonstrations, and perhaps the occasional referendum thus all contribute to the improvement of communication between Them and Us. But They on their side must be not only willing to listen, but also competent to perform the tasks imposed on them – competent, that is to say, to handle the growing complexity of issues which I have listed as the third of the obstacles which contemporary democracy has to negotiate. Here the traditional amateurism of the British (and indeed many other) systems of government may well raise doubts. Amateur status, which appears to be rapidly disappearing from the world of sport, paradoxically survives almost unimpaired in the machinery of government. Not only do Ministers usually lack any specific qualifications relevant to the work of the Departments over which they preside: it must also be admitted that it would make very little difference if they were so qualified, such is the agility with which they are expected to leap from one Department to another.

The periodic Cabinet reshuffle seems to have become almost a constitutional convention. Thus, the only Cabinet Ministers who held the same office continuously throughout the Labour Government of 1966–70 were the Prime Minister, the Lord Chancellor, the Secretary of State for Scotland (Mr Ross) and the Chief Secretary to the Treasury, Mr Diamond. Mr Michael Stewart's first tenure of office as Foreign Secretary was interrupted after four months by a year as Secretary of State for Economic Affairs, after which he returned to the Foreign Office, with which seven months later the Department of Commonwealth Affairs was amalgamated. After twenty months in their respective offices as Home Secretary and Chancellor of the Exchequer, Mr Jenkins and Mr Callaghan stepped into each other's shoes. At the Ministry of Transport, horses were changed in mid-stream when Mrs Castle departed to become Secretary for Employment and Productivity, leaving her successor, Mr Richard Marsh, to pilot an extremely complicated Bill in the final stages of its voyage through the Commons. Within two years Mr Marsh was himself thrown out of the Government altogether, his place being taken by Mr Fred Mulley. Mr Anthony Greenwood made his début as Minister of Overseas Development, then moved to the Ministry of Housing and Local Government, where he was later deprived of Cabinet rank. Shortly after this demotion he resigned, and was succeeded for the last few weeks of the Government's life by Mr William Mellish who had no time to do more than make one or two bold speeches. Progressive demotion was also the fate of Mr Kenneth Robinson, who, after more than two years as Minister of Health, was transferred to a somewhat anomalous position as Minister of Land and Planning in the Ministry of Housing and Local Government from which he too disappeared in a matter of months. By contrast Mr Roy Mason had a meteoric rise from nine months as Minister of State, Board of Trade, to Minister of Defence for Equipment (fifteen months), and thereafter to Paymaster-General, Minister of Power and President of the Board of Trade, all within two years. Mr Crossman also, as befits his reputation for a highly volatile temperament, had a strikingly varied career. After four months as Minister of Housing, he served for over two years as Lord President of the Council and leader of the House of Commons, and was then transferred to the Ministry of Health, subsequently expanded into the Department of Health and Social Security.

Within the framework of our constitution specialist Ministers can only be exceptional; nor do Prime Ministers show much enthusiasm to make use of such as are available. Mr Wilson did indeed give the Department of Education and Science to a teacher, and chose a doctor for a junior post at the Department of Health and Social Security; but successive Governments have shown great reluctance to appoint a medically qualified Minister of Health. In any case, however, only a few professions are likely to be represented in Parliament, and there is therefore unlikely to be any great wealth of talent upon which to draw. Nor has the practice of using timely by-elections to introduce outsiders been conspicuously successful: Ministers have to be politicians and Parliamentarians as well as Departmental Heads, and the outsider with no Parliamentary experience may well be at a loss in these roles. There is moreover a case against, as well as a case for, the specialist Minister. It could well be argued that any doctor in charge of the Department of Health would be bound to be committed on many of the controversial issues that come within the purview of that Ministry. Ministers, it is said, even more than those who serve them, ought to be, in the Fulton idiom, 'generalists'.

But can there be any justification in the contemporary world for the instability of ministerial tenure of office which has become customary? Mr Wilson's games of general post were by no means exceptional. They could be rivalled by previous Tory administrations, and, I think, even surpassed by some. One can understand that a Minister who did not shine in one office might quite quickly be demoted or moved to another. But a career as meteoric as that of Mr Roy Mason is very hard to reconcile with the simple theory that people generally do a job better when they know something about it. At the best of times, when a new Government takes over, Ministers are likely in the first days of office to have to make decisions on matters about which they know nothing. Why multiply these situations unnecessarily?

It will of course be said that such decisions (and perhaps a good many others also, even when the Minister is more seasoned) are made by him only in name. He does what his Civil Servants tell him to do. But the disquieting feature here is that the mobility of the Higher Civil Service is second only to that of Ministers. A survey instigated by the Fulton Committee revealed that the administrators interviewed (other than assistant principals) had held their current positions for an average of only 2·7 years and had averaged no more than 2·8 years in all their completed jobs. For executive officers in Administrative Divisions the average duration was 4·1 years.[7]

Some of this mobility is no doubt due to promotion, and may not mean breaking into quite new fields; but not all. For example, a civil servant who has been heavily involved in legislation on town and country planning has been moved from the Ministry of Housing and Local Government to be head of the Prison Department at the Home Office; while another planning officer took charge of Mr Wilson's Secretariat at 10, Downing Street, lost this job owing to the change of Government, and returned, not to the exercise of his skill as a planner, but to a post concerned with Community Relations. Again, Sir Philip Allen has been successively Second Secretary at the Treasury and Under-Secretary of State at the Home Office; and Sir John Maud, as he then was, after seven years' experience in the top job at the Ministry of Education had to sacrifice this specialist experience on transfer to a similar position at the Ministry of Power. Sometimes it would seem that the more exalted the position, the more insecure the tenure.

Undoubtedly there are common elements in the art of administration which are independent of what is administered; and the civil servants who glide so smoothly from one post to another claim that this is the art which they practise. Likewise

[7] Committee on the Civil Service 1966–8, Vol. 2, *Evidence, Report of a Management Consultancy Group*, pp. 20, 28.

company directors may exercise the same financial skill in fixing take-over bids or other stock market manœuvres, regardless of whether their companies make tractors or plastic macs. But the point is that government is more than administration: government involves also questions of policy. The staff of the prison service must advise Ministers on such matters as prison security, or the desirability of retaining, modifying or abolishing the present Borstal system. Personal brilliance may complement, but is hardly an adequate substitute for, experience of such questions, to which concentrated study of the law relating to town and country planning would seem to have little relevance. In the words of the Fulton Committee: 'It cannot make for the efficient despatch of public business when key men rarely stay in one job longer than two or three years before being moved to some other post, often in a very different area of government activity.'[8] One can, indeed, only be thankful that in a few areas the hiving off of commercial functions to public corporations has at least guaranteed some measure of continuity. Does anyone doubt that the coal industry has been more efficiently managed under Lord Robens' ten years' direction than it would have been under a succession of Ministers, served perhaps by an equally rapid succession of Permanent Secretaries?

The unwillingness of the Civil Service to value expertise, moreover, goes even further than this. It is inherent also in the salary structure of the service. Research officers employed in posts for which they have specialist qualifications are paid substantially less than the corresponding administrative grades; and they also lack any prospect of reaching the top jobs. As the Management Consultancy Group, which investigated these matters for the Fulton Committee, expressed it

[8] Ibid. *Report*, p. 11.

with engaging candour: 'Since Assistant Principals, in contrast to Assistant Research Officers, do not usually have qualifications or experience appropriate to the work of the Department, this amounts to discrimination against expertise'.[9] In the Committee's own words 'many scientists, engineers and members of other specialist classes get neither the full responsibilities and corresponding authority, nor the opportunities they ought to have'.[10]

Meanwhile a new threat to traditional amateurism and to faith in intuitive judgement and generalized administrative experience is making an appearance on the not-so-distant horizon. In the age of the computer, decisions that involve the evaluation of extremely complex data may be more efficiently dealt with by electronic than by human means. But the acceptance and the exploitation of this possibility demands an outlook far removed from that of the typical Oxbridge Arts graduate in the higher civil service. In a recent paperback Mr Michael Rose has drawn a vivid picture of the effect of computerization upon the prestige, and indeed the self-confidence, of administrators and managers in both government and industry; and he is the more convincing inasmuch as he does not regard the computer as the universal passport to salvation. What Mr Rose predicts of the attitudes of the typical business manager to the new techniques is likely to be no less applicable to the administrator in national or local government. 'His traditionalism, departmental outlook, suspicion of experts, preference of experience to theory, and improvising approach make him naturally hostile to computing and system concepts and computer personnel. It all sounds like high-flown nonsense which will merely upset day-to-day routine. The idea that he

[9] Ibid., Vol. 2, *Evidence*, p. 41.
[10] Ibid., *Report*, p. 12.

should familiarize himself with the new techniques, or that someone in his job will in future depend on them, is an affront to his whole outlook and set of personal values.'[11] Perhaps the measure of the change in background and training that the new era will demand may be inferred from the fact that in 1965 out of 125 successful entrants into the administrative class of the civil service, only four had degrees in mathematics and ten in science and technology, as against forty-five who had graduated in history.[12] Such are the men and women who in fifteen or twenty years' time will be holding the top civil service jobs.

V

Within the compass of a single lecture you will not expect me to provide a blueprint which will resolve all the tribulations of contemporary democracy, though I hope that in passing I have been able to indicate some developments and inventions which give ground for at least a qualified optimism. I am, however, conscious of an obligation to suggest one or two more fundamental changes which appear to be essential to the health, and perhaps even to the survival, of political democracy.

First, the line between ends and means needs to be redrawn. Admittedly, it is easier to say this than to indicate just where the line should go. But the basic principle is that the ends of political activity are matters for the layman's judgement, whereas the means of achieving those ends are not. To illustrate: we can all form an image of the kind of society in which we would prefer to live. Some of us set a high value on social and

[11] Rose, Michael, *Computers, Managers and Society* (Pelican Books, 1969), p. 245.
[12] Committee on the Civil Service 1966–8, Vol. IV, *Evidence*, p. 323.

economic equality and would like to see the gap between rich and poor narrowed rather than (as is happening at present) growing even wider. We dislike privilege in all its guises: we think it more important that everybody should have enough than that some should have superabundance. Others set great store on the competitive struggle as a stimulus to energy and enterprise. To them increasing prosperity matters more than the way in which the fruits thereof are distributed. Again, to some of us soldiering is at best a disagreeable but possibly unavoidable adjunct of contemporary civilization, and the less of it we can do with, the better. Others are ready to glorify what they call the Honourable Profession of Arms.

Such examples of profound differences in the ultimate social values cherished by individuals within our community could be multiplied indefinitely; but less and less are they the stuff of which politics are made. In the early years of this century, perhaps even as late as the General Election of 1945, the ultimate objectives of the political parties – their respective conceptions of the Good Society – were clearly distinguishable, and the layman chose between them largely in accordance with his own moral standards. But in the past twenty-five years or so the parties appear to have lost sight of their distinctive social philosophies, and to have sought only to be judged by their efficiency in running everything more or less according to the established pattern. Since the 1970 election things may perhaps be changing, but up till then the voter has been consulted, not on ends, but on technical questions of means, such as stop–go economic policies or devaluation, which are most unlikely to be within his competence; and at the same time he has had little opportunity of expressing his preference as to the kind of world that he desires for himself and his children. It is as though the passengers in a train had no longer any say in its destination, but were only consulted about its speed or the technicalities of the heating system.

Moreover, one of the oddities of the present situation is that the issues on which the average citizen is most likely to be competent to give an opinion are the very ones on which he is least likely to be consulted. Typical of these are questions relating to 'permissive' legislation, which raise moral rather than technical issues. Under the present curious procedure, however, governments take no responsibility for legislation on these topics, preferring to leave them for the individual MP to decide according to his conscience – with the result that they have no place in the alternative political programmes with which the elector is presented.

My second condition for the promotion of democratic health is that there should be frank admission of priorities. In our personal lives we all know that, for reasons of money or time or more probably both, it is impossible to do everything that we wish to do at once. Yet I cannot recall any election in which the Parties explicitly indicated the order in which they ranked their various proposals, distinguishing what we might expect them to tackle immediately from what they hoped would come later, if circumstances should permit. Suppose that in the 1970 election the Labour Party had said 'If re-elected our first task will be to abolish poverty. This will mean immediate increases in family allowances, National Insurance Benefits and Supplementary Benefit, and will take precedence over all other claims for additional public expenditure. After that our next priority will be housing: slums and homelessness are anachronisms and we will not tolerate their continuance. Our other proposals will take second place to these urgent necessities.' Such a declaration would have struck an entirely new note of realism, as Mr Heath might likewise have done, had he given some indication of when and where tax reductions might be expected and in what areas expenditure would first be reduced. But our political leaders seem unable to realize that their persistent disregard of priorities is an insult to the electorate, and only feeds the cynicism with which they are too often regarded.

My third and final condition is in effect another facet of the same principle. The layman cannot pass intelligent judgement on a miscellany of proposals unless he is alive to costs and alternatives; and by this I do not necessarily mean costs as expressed in monetary terms. To take a highly topical example, every proposed site for a third London airport has met with strong local opposition, as have also many plans for extensions of motorways. Public resistance to the noise of aircraft and to the death, destruction and pollution disseminated by motor vehicles is growing rapidly; but sooner or later, and sooner rather than later, it must be realized that these nuisances are the price to be paid for the right to travel speedily and at a not too great expense all over the world. I said earlier that it is a mistake to suppose that the complex of conflicting interests, which is one of the major problems of contemporary society, is always a conflict between different persons. It may well be a conflict within one and the same person. If an airport is objectionable wherever it goes, it is no solution merely to try to get it sited somewhere else: the objector must ask himself what price in the reduction of air transport facilities he himself would be willing to pay in order to be free of the misery which its proximity inflicts. Would he, for example, be prepared to forego his Continenta package holiday? And is the motorway opponent prepared to face the possibility of future restrictions upon the use, or even the private ownership, of cars?

In other words, it is time that we grew up – and that goes for politician and voter alike. The trouble about democratic decisions is that they tend to be made in an atmosphere of omnipotent fantasy, rather than realistically as choices between alternatives. The politician conceals the fact that every item in his programme competes with every other for manpower and money; and the citizen presses for this proposal and objects to that, with scant regard to alternatives or consequences. Such childish posturings seem to be a characteristic peculiarity of political life: most of us have outgrown them in relation to our personal affairs. Only in politics is a comparable maturity of attitude, on the part of both rulers and ruled, long overdue.

3

DEVIANCE, CRIMINAL AND OTHER

I

Since this lecture will be largely concerned with criminal behaviour and its causes and treatment, I must make it plain at the outset that, although I am a member of the Home Office Penal Advisory Council, everything that I say, except when quoting the Council's published Reports, is an expression of my personal views for which the Council has no responsibility.

Before, however, we plunge into criminology, something must be said about British attitudes to, and tolerance of, non-criminal deviance. Such toleration is of two kinds: tolerance of verbal utterances, and of other forms of behaviour. In the former we rank pretty high, at least by comparison with much of the rest of the world, although our racial tolerance is still so insecure that attempts have had to be made to enforce it by law. In politics generally, however, Northern Ireland and some demonstrations excepted, physical violence is extremely rare: Members of Parliament who indulge in furious verbal battles on the floor of the House are remarkably matey behind the scenes. In religious observance likewise actual persecution is no longer practised. Even the professedly religious battles between Catholics and Protestants in Northern Ireland are at least as much political as sectarian. Each side may hate the other's theological doctrines; but Catholics are equally resentful of the political disabilities imposed upon them – in employment, in housing and even in voting rights – while Protestants fight to retain their privileged position. Nevertheless it is still true throughout the United Kingdom that the Christian Churches' hold on the mass media denies any comparable opportunities for publicity to the exponents of alternative, and, in particular, agnostic philosophies.

Tolerance, though widely acclaimed as a virtue is admirable only within limits. We are tolerant (and rightly so) only on subjects that we do not think greatly matter. Anyone who *really* believed, as one believes that day will follow night, that a child who rejects the Christian religion will burn till all eternity in Dante's hell would be bound passionately to resist the agnostic's claim to preach disbelief. Hence the growth of religious tolerance in this country is, I suggest, simply a reflection of the decline in religious conviction of which I gave some evidence in my first lecture. The fact that the blasphemy laws are falling into disuse, while new legislation prohibits incitement to racial hatred, is proof that God now matters less than coloured people.

Political tolerance likewise, not to say apathy, may be explained by the fact that Party-political controversies, at least until the 1970 election, appeared to be degenerating into shadow-boxing. Nevertheless political toleration seems to be less secure than its religious counterpart. It is constantly under threat from demonstrators; nor do recent events abroad encourage complacency. Perhaps the truth is that in this country most of us do not care enough about politics: if we cared more, political controversies would soon be much less tolerantly conducted.

In relation to non-verbal forms of deviance also, the British record of toleration ranks relatively high; though not, I think, as high as in the spheres of party politics and religion. In the past few years the characteristic patterns of non-criminal deviance in this country have undergone some striking changes. Not so long ago the typical deviants were the spivs and the wide-boys, out for themselves and on the make to get every penny that they could out of a commercially-minded environment. They sought to exploit, each man for himself, not to reject, our acquisitive, competitive society. But today the typical deviant is the hippy or the drop-out, for whom, not exploitation, but total rejection of accepted standards, is the rule; and towards him tolerance is so far from securely founded that even trivial irrelevancies evoke strong passions. Who can seriously suggest that the wearing of long hair or exotic styles of dress is a mortal sin? Yet from the fuss made by headmasters and parents up and down the country, one would imagine that it was. And to plead in exculpation that these eccentricities are damaging to a young man's earthly career is merely to testify to the intolerance of potential employers.

The protest of the hippy, equally with that of the spiv, is a reaction against established values; and the fury aroused by hair styles springs from recognition that these are merely symbols of this reaction. Yet attacks upon symbols that are innocuous in themselves are apt, by their very irrationality, to rebound upon their authors; nor, as I suggested in my opening lecture, are the merits of the acquisitive society so conspicuous that the challenge that lies behind the symbols deserves to be denied expression. If the choice is between the values of the hippy and those of the Pentagon, where do you and I take our stand?

Always the demands for conformity in contemporary

society exercise relentless pressure; and they are constantly reinforced from new quarters. In the United States, and to a less extent in this country also, a sinister trend in recent years has been the identification of conformity with mental health. As long ago as 1938 Professor Kingsley Davis pronounced the American concept of mental health to be strongly coloured by the ideals of the 'free enterprise' society, embodied in a moral system which 'accepts social advancement as a natural goal' and regards lack of ambition as a 'definite symptom of maladjustment'; in which 'behaviour should manifest prudence, rationality and foresight, and material possessions should not be dissipated by whimsical extravagance'; and in which enjoyment, though not frowned upon, must be 'wholesome'.[1] Again, in 1965 another American, Dr H. Warren Dunham wrote that mental sickness is today ascribed to practically every type of deviant behaviour, such as 'delinquents, sex offenders, alcoholics, drug addicts, beatniks, Communists, the racially prejudiced and, in fact, practically all persons who do not fit into the prevailing togetherness that we like to think characterizes middle-class American life';[2] while one of the contributors to a review of various concepts of mental health by the Scientific Committee of the World Federation for Mental Health has gone so far as to assert that mental health 'demands good interpersonal relations with oneself, with others, and with God' – a definition which, as that relentless critic of this trend, Dr Thomas Szasz, points out 'neatly places all atheists in the class of the mentally sick'.[3]

[1] Davis, Kingsley, 'Mental Hygiene and the Class Structure', *Psychiatry*, February 1938, *1*, 55–65.
[2] Dunham, H. Warren, 'Community Psychiatry: the newest therapeutic bandwagon', *International Journal of Psychiatry*, *1*, 553, 1965.
[3] Szasz, Thomas S, *Ideology and Insanity* (Doubleday & Co. Inc., New York, 1970), p. 36.

These developments are the more alarming in so far as they have succeeded in enlisting the prestige of the medical profession in the cause of social conformism. It is indeed disturbing to learn that the University of Harvard holds a weekly 'medical administrative' lunch, attended by the psychiatric and other medical and surgical staff of the University, representatives from the student counselling service – and the Chief of the University Police.[4]

Meanwhile, Professor Gerald Caplan, himself an emigrant from this country, has advocated the appointment of 'community psychiatrists' who are to focus, not only on 'previously or currently mentally disordered persons, but on those who may become sick'. For this purpose psychiatrists are to carry their activities into 'such fields as education, welfare, recreation, urban planning and religion'; and they are to establish themselves as persons 'who can give politicians added understanding of the human needs of their members'. Indeed they have only to 'convince the medical authorities in the clinics' that their 'operations are a logical extension of traditional medical practice' for their 'role to be sanctioned by all concerned'. Already mental health specialists in the USA are being consulted 'to help the legislators and welfare authorities improve the moral[5] atmosphere' in the homes where illegitimate children are being brought up and 'to influence their mothers to marry and provide them with stable fathers'.[6] But what perhaps more than anything else gives the game away, and betrays identification of mental health with particular moral and social attitudes is Professor Caplan's declaration that 'a psychiatrist

[4] Ibid. p. 156.
[5] Italics mine – B.W.
[6] Caplan, Gerald, *Principles of Preventive Psychiatry* (Tavistock Publications, 1964), pp. 270, 66, 64, 79, 89.

whose political views are on the extreme right would have a hard time working with a left-wing political party', while 'a pacifist psychiatrist would have difficulty working in the army'.[7] Who has ever heard of a right-wing surgeon finding any moral difficulty in removing the appendix of a left-wing politician, or a pacifist physician being unable conscientiously to administer anti-biotics to a general suffering from pneumonia? If the mental health which the community psychiatrists are to promote is as objective as its physical counterpart, why do these moral difficulties arise in the one case and not in the other? It is indeed hardly surprising that in one case in which a group of mental health experts descended uninvited upon a community, educating them 'in a highly organized way on the nature of mental disorder and its manifestations', the population ended with 'more negative attitudes towards the mental health problem than before', and 'developed marked feelings of hostility toward the mental health workers who had disturbed the orderly processes of their community'.[8]

Things have not yet come to such a pass in this country. Recently, however, Professor Henry Miller has thought it necessary to remind his colleagues that a psychiatrist is 'one who treats mental illness' not one who 'prevents wars, cures anti-Semitism, offers to transform the normally abrasive relations between men into a tedium of stultifying harmony, is the ultimate authority on bringing up children or selecting managing directors – or misuses his jargon to pronounce on every issue of the day in an incessant series of television appearances'.[9] Moreover talk of 'preventive' social action may not infre-

[7] Ibid., p. 65.
[8] Ibid., p. 182.
[9] Miller, Henry, 'The Abuse of Psychiatry', *Encounter*, XXXIV, May 5, 1970.

quently be heard where psychiatrists and social workers are gathered together. Even the seemingly innocent section of the 1963 Children and Young Persons Act, which lays upon Local Authorities the duty to make available advice, guidance and assistance in order to keep children out of the juvenile courts could be used to impose standards of conformism stricter than those laid down by law; and the 1959 Mental Health Act, if broadly interpreted (which, happily, it has not so far been) would allow any adolescent who persists in 'seriously irresponsible' or 'abnormally aggressive' behaviour to be diagnosed, and indeed detained, as a 'psychopath'. How many motor-cyclists might not be caught in this net?

Language, moreover, is often revealing. On both sides of the Atlantic mental health is apt to be equated with the absence of what is called 'emotional disturbance'. Yet all the successful reforms in the world have been instigated by powerful emotional drives and all reformers have been motivated by emotional disturbances. Under any identification of psychological health with emotional calm or with 'adjustment' (to use another favourite psychiatric term) Charles Bradlaugh, Florence Nightingale, E. D. Morel and Emmeline Pankhurst would all certainly have qualified as in need of psychiatric treatment.

Freedom is precious to the individual: and a society with a wide variety of cultural standards and deviant behaviour offers a far richer and more colourful life than one which is rigidly conformist. In the complex modern world a vast array of controls and prohibitions is indisputably necessary in the public interest; and these must be clearly defined and enforced by law. This in itself makes it the more necessary to preserve the utmost liberty outside of this prohibited area. But the danger is, I think, that, between the white area of personal freedom and the black area of conduct legally prohibited, there should come to be a nebulous intermediate zone in which various social pressures seek to impose uniformity. Either idleness, promiscuity, drunkenness and a generally disorganized way of life must be accepted even by those to whom they are distasteful, or they should be forbidden by law. Psychiatrists, social workers and Mrs Mary Whitehouse notwithstanding, the non-criminal deviant has his rights, and these must be respected.

II

And now what of the deviants who infringe the criminal law? To begin with the facts.[10] Detected crime has been increasing with only occasional fluctuations ever since the first world war. In 1969 the total of indictable crimes known to the police was 1,488,638: whereas for the years 1920–29 the annual average was 117,239 and for 1930–39 231,025. That means an increase of about 12½ times since the decade following the first world war, and a more than six-fold rise over the annual average for the decade immediately preceding Hitler's war. Such figures are plainly out of all proportion to the increase in population in the same periods. In the past twenty years, there have only been three occasions when the total of crimes known to the police fell below the figure for the immediately preceding year: these were 1952 with a drop of 2·1 per cent, 1953 with 7·9 per cent and 1954 with 8·2 per cent. The hopes thus raised, however, were thereafter dashed and have never since been revived, since from 1955 to 1969 the rise has been continuous, though the rate of increase has been very variable. During the past twenty

---

[10] The figures in this section are derived from the (annual) *Criminal Statistics*, the (annual) *Return of Offences Relating to Motor Vehicles* and the *Reports of the Prison Department of the Home Office* (HMSO).

years the total of detected indictable crimes has in fact more than trebled, rising from 461,435 in 1950 to the 1969 figure of 1,488,638. Known crimes of violence, moreover, have risen twice as fast even as this, with a six-fold increase from 6,249 in 1950 to 37,818 in 1969.

Only a minority of offenders who perpetrate these crimes is ever brought to book. In 1969 the proportion of known indictable crimes 'cleared up' was only 42·1 per cent, and has actually fallen since 1950 when it stood at 46·6 per cent. Even so, however, the total of persons convicted is formidable enough. In 1969 the number of convictions for indictable crimes stood at 304,070 (116,021 in 1950); and to these may be added the numbers convicted of non-indictable offences, which in 1969 reached the handsome figure of 1,302,658, thus giving a grand total of 1,606,728 found guilty by the Courts – not far short of two and a half times the 1950 figure of 688,650. With a population of about 40,747,000 at risk in England and Wales, this means that at the present rate nearly one in every twenty-five of us must expect to acquire a conviction in a criminal court every year.

Please do not imagine, however, that everyone convicted of an indictable offence corresponds to the popular stereotype of a criminal. All stealing is indictable and the figures of indictable crimes are swollen by a very large number of quite modest thefts. Amongst the non-indictable offenders, motorists have for many years constituted by far the largest number. In 1969, they were responsible for almost 59 per cent of all criminal convictions for crimes great or small, a proportion which, though higher than the 1950 figure of 52·6 per cent, has been falling slightly in the past few years. Indeed, if anyone is searching for a small crumb of comfort in the generally accelerating torrent of criminal convictions, he may perhaps find it in the fact that the number of persons convicted of motoring offences which had long been rising has actually now fallen from 1,046,876 in 1967 to 979,054 in 1969. If only motorists would keep up the good work! So long as they constitute over half the cases dealt with by the courts, the drain on police resources is extremely formidable. The motoring community could indeed make a magnificent contribution to the reduction of crime in general, if they would conscientiously observe all the provisions of the Road Traffic Acts, thus enabling the great body of police now engaged in prosecuting traffic offenders to turn their attention to other forms of crime.

Meanwhile, even in the constantly rising volume of indictable convictions, some relatively stable features still remain. Eleven years ago I wrote that if men behaved like women and boys behaved like girls, the courts would be idle and the prisons empty. This is still true, though the gap between the sexes appears to be very slowly narrowing. Before the war in 1938, male outdistanced female convictions per 100,000 of population at all ages by 7·7 to 1. In 1950 the corresponding figure stood at 7·3 to 1; and in 1969 it had fallen to 7·2. Moreover, what is true, as between the sexes, is likewise true as between the young and the not so young. If the young behaved like their elders, once again the courts and the prisons would be nearly out of business. In 1950 the peak number of each sex found guilty of indictable offences per 100,000 at risk reached its maximum at the age of fourteen; and fourteen was still the peak age, in 1968, though in 1969 for some unexplained reason it rose to seventeen. From these youthful peaks, the proportion of convictions drops steadily with advancing years. In 1950 out of every 100,000 males at risk 2,303 were convicted at the age of fourteen as against 449 at ages between thirty and forty, a drop of 80 per cent; and this was followed by an even greater

75

reduction at later ages. For 1969 the drop from the peak at seventeen is about 75 per cent, and at both dates the trend for females is similar though the reduction is less dramatic. To those who shake their heads over this lamentable evidence of the wickedness of the young, let me offer this small consolation: at least it looks as if most youthful offenders eventually learn the error of their ways. Indeed the improvement must be even better than these figures suggest, since the totals for the later ages include a number of late entrants to the world of crime. Nor can this concentration of convictions at early ages be a mark of the deteriorating morality of the present generation. Right back before the war the concentration of detected crimes upon the young was at least as great as it is today.

Such then is the picture, in face of which everybody is asking what has gone wrong and what can we do about it? The answers to those questions must, I think, be sought on two levels. First, how much responsibility lies at the door of our penal system? and, second, what more fundamental changes in the quality of our society today encourage defiance of the criminal law? At neither level, unfortunately, are demonstrably valid answers yet to hand. But at least one widely accepted answer is patently wrong; and for the rest we all have our hypotheses. About my own hypotheses I shall have something to say presently.

In the meantime the one definitely wrong answer can be quickly disposed of. This attributes the increase in crime, particularly crime of a violent nature, to the abolition of the death penalty. But this *must* be wrong, if only because, as the official figures show, detected crime has been on the increase for fully half a century, while the rise in crimes of violence has been exceptionally dramatic for the past twenty years or more; yet the death penalty has only been wholly in abeyance since

1965 and in restricted use since 1957. Its abolition *cannot* therefore, have anything to do with trends that were well established many decades earlier. The murder rate in this country has indeed remained astonishingly stable. Throughout the whole of this century the decennial average has ranged only between 3·2 and 4·5 per million of population,[11] with minor, and apparently fortuitous, fluctuations which certainly have had nothing to do with the comings and goings of the death penalty.

Nevertheless our penal system (along with many if not most of the penal systems of the world) may well be judged a dismal failure. But then it is required to tackle an impossible job. First, it is in the position of locking the stable door after the horse has bolted – attempting, that is to say, to prevent crimes after they have been committed. The penal authorities are in fact faced with much the same problem as doctors trying to cure any of the forms of cancer for which no reliable remedy is known. Even though in many cases a single operation for cancer may be successful, the chances that a second will be required are greater than if the first had not been necessary. Similarly, to have had one conviction (even if a fair proportion, though seldom a majority, of offenders do not repeat their offences) increases the chances of a second; and the second increases still further the chances of a third – and so on for quite a long sequence. Without inferring (although in some penal cases this is probably true) that the treatment actually aggravates the subject's condition, we must admit that it is often ineffectual. We just do not know what to do.

Secondly penal treatment is required to achieve multiple objectives which may well be mutually incompatible. As a

[11] Including, since 1957, cases of manslaughter with diminished responsibility which would presumably have been previously classed as murder.

magistrate with forty-four years' experience behind me, I cannot but be acutely conscious of these conflicts. Ideally, the sentence passed on an offender should simultaneously (1) teach him to desist from further criminality, (2) deter others from imitating him, (3) keep him out of harm's way, if he is likely to be a danger to the community. Yet, quite apart from the fact that we are hopelessly in the dark as to the effectiveness of deterrence upon the community at large, there is good reason to suspect that many offenders – the so-called 'inadequates' – will never keep out of trouble unless they enjoy actually *better* conditions than they could ever expect to achieve for themselves; and the spectacle of the criminal being apparently rewarded, rather than punished, for his crimes is hardly likely to discourage his potential imitators.

However, even an impossible job can often be done better or worse; and here I would like to offer three suggestions. First it is absolutely imperative that the prison population must be reduced. There are at present about 40,000 men and about 1,000 women confined in prisons, borstals or detention centres – a total which involves crowding into the local prisons at least 50 per cent more than these institutions were built to accommodate. Such overcrowding necessarily puts immense obstacles in the way of the introduction of anything that can be called a constructive regime. In most of our penal institutions the staffs are overwhelmed by the day-to-day problems of coping with impossible numbers. Indeed it is astonishing that so many of them nevertheless retain their enthusiasm and still cherish the image of a system which, in the words of the first of the present official prison Rules, would 'encourage and assist' prisoners 'to lead a good and useful life'. The tragedy is that the greater the numbers who pass through our prisons, the more hopelessly out of touch with reality does this admirable objective become. Certainly the figures of reconvictions bear melancholy witness to the failure of imprisonment to encourage anything like a 'good and useful life'. More than half the men sentenced to eighteen months or more are reconvicted within two years, as are over two-thirds of those who have served sentences of four years and upwards; and for young offenders the figures are particularly discouraging. About 70 per cent of young men who have served Borstal sentences are reconvicted within three years, and for young prisoners on licence after sentences of over three months, the figure rises to 75 per cent.[12]

The problem of devising alternatives to imprisonment is therefore a matter of great urgency. On this a Sub-Committee of the Home Office Penal Advisory Council[13] has recently put forward some new proposals, the most 'imaginative and hopeful' of which, in the Council's own estimation, is the suggestion that the courts should be empowered to require offenders to carry out service to the community in their spare time. Already several voluntary organizations undertake a variety of services, such as constructing adventure playgrounds, clearing beaches and footpaths, helping in hospital wards and kitchens and in clubs for the physically disabled. It is now proposed that in suitable cases offenders might be required to participate in these activities, working, as far as may be practicable, alongside the present volunteers. While not precisely defining the categories of offender upon whom this obligation might be imposed, the Sub-Committee suggested that it might be appropriate for some cases of theft, for persons guilty of the unauthorized use of motor vehicles, for the more serious traffic

---

[12] *People in Prison* (HMSO, 1969, Cmnd 4214), p. 53.
[13] Advisory Council on the Penal System, *Report on Non-Custodial and Semi-Custodial Penalties* (HMSO, 1970).

offenders, and for some cases of malicious damage and minor assaults.

These proposals would require fresh legislation, nor could they, in any case, be brought into operation immediately throughout the whole country: the scheme would have to be introduced in the first instance experimentally in those areas where active voluntary organizations are already engaged in community service. The members of the Sub-Committee were, however, greatly encouraged by the cordial reception which their proposal received both from representatives of the voluntary associations concerned and from the probation service. The former were confident that they could find plenty of suitable tasks on which offenders could be engaged and that there would be no serious difficulties in employing them alongside volunteers. Indeed informal arrangements have already occasionally been made under which prisoners or probationers are allowed to join volunteers in community service. Representatives of the probation service, on their side also, expressed the utmost readiness to act as intermediaries between the courts and the voluntary agencies in making the detailed arrangements for the offender's initial placement and for continuing contact with him.

Is it too much to hope that in the not-so-distant future the great majority of offenders will remain within the community, either under obligation to spend their leisure in a prescribed form of public service, or residing, under supervision, in hostels from which they would go to work outside in the ordinary way? Prison sentences would then be reserved for the small number with really serious anti-social tendencies for which no successful treatment has yet been discovered.

So long, however, as prisons, Borstals and detention centres continue to be thronged with thousands of thieves, robbers, burglars and vandals – most of whom will eventually settle down – far more attention needs to be paid to the reshaping of the typical prison regime. That is the objective of my second proposal. Here the real problem is to break down the artificiality and irrelevance which beset all totally segregated institutions, and prisons more than most; and this problem, moreover, is by no means confined to any one type of penal regime. In the rigidly disciplined life of traditional prisons, the inmate has no opportunity to make even the smallest personal decisions: he is generally badly under-occupied, while such work as he is required to do is likely to be monotonous and unrewarding; and he is lucky indeed if he gets any real help from the prison staff. In short, little or nothing is done to induce him to see the error of his previous ways or to strengthen his hand against future temptations. But in the more progressive modern institutions also, total segregation has its problems. In those that are psychiatrically orientated, the prisoner may have ample opportunity to let off steam and to air the innumerable grievances and injustices by which the typical recidivist likes to excuse his conduct. Yet, in the world outside, keeping out of trouble more often means bottling up one's steam rather than letting it off. Moreover, the more civilized of our prisons and Borstals are staffed by sympathetic people who treat their charges with consideration and respect, and often with quite astonishing patience. Thus, at least so far as is humanly possible, prisoners are screened from the bullying foreman or the would-be partner in crime, not to mention all the financial anxieties and the inevitable conflicts of domestic life. Clearly the therapeutic community must be very nice to live in, but is it good practice for life in the wicked world outside?

Fundamentally, I think, the problems here are insoluble: the most intractable weakness of any institutional regime, punitive or therapeutic, is that it cannot mirror either the responsibilities or the temptations of ordinary life. But there can be degrees of irrelevance. The only open girls' Borstal in the country, many of whose inmates presumably come from the slums of the great conurbations, provides a basic training only in farm work, although a somewhat old-fashioned type of embroidery reminiscent of Victorian samplers is also taught. Some of these young women take to country life and get jobs on the land when they leave; but one wonders what their months of this training do for those who go back whence they came. Today it is still exceptional for the vocational training given in any penal institution to be subsequently put to serious use. Still more exceptional is the institution which is more concerned to focus its inmates' attention upon their own problems, and upon those which they create for society, than to keep them occupied in washing stone floors or breaking down old radios in the intervals of long periods of boring idleness. Nevertheless times are changing. Group counselling is an advance on sewing mailbags. Some day perhaps it will be given as large a place in the picture.

My third proposal relates only to children. I think it quite wrong for children of compulsory school age to be dealt with in a court of law – even a juvenile court – except in cases of homicide. What is the function of an educational system, unless to bring up the young in the way they should go? Although legislation is already on the statute book which categorically forbids any criminal charge (except homicide) being brought against a child under fourteen, this is not yet in force; and I doubt if it will make any real difference when it is, since a child will still be liable to be found 'guilty of an offence' under a civil procedure – a distinction which is most unlikely to be understood by any but a handful of the children and their parents who appear before the courts.

My fundamental objections to any juvenile court proceedings involving children of school age are threefold. First, no matter how conscientiously the magistrates try to make the language and the atmosphere informal, the rules of procedure which the court is obliged to observe are altogether too rigid for children to understand, or to be applied to them. Second, children should be dealt with by people with whom they are in contact in their normal day-to-day lives, and not by strangers upon whom they have never before set eyes: if they will respond to anybody it is to those whom they know and perhaps respect, and may even love. And, third, and most important of all, a child against whom a court order is made, no matter whether the proceedings are criminal or civil, inevitably acquires a delinquent label and is initiated into a delinquent culture. I am sure that for this very reason many a child leaves the juvenile court more, rather than less, likely to embark upon a criminal career. In the busy courts of the big cities, probably more delinquents are made in the waiting-room than are ever unmade in the court itself.

After all, the 'special educational treatment' which local authorities are statutorily required to provide for children who need it is pretty comprehensive. It can include remedial classes, boarding schools, schools for the educationally sub-normal, the maladjusted and the physically handicapped, not to mention child guidance clinics; while the Mental Health Act makes provision for the mentally subnormal and the psychotic child. Even if these facilities look more impressive on paper than in reality, they could be greatly extended if the staff and other resources now employed in juvenile courts and approved schools were transferred to them. Surely they are varied enough to cater for every type of child and for every childhood problem?

I would hope, therefore, that much criminality might be nipped in the bud, if children of school age were not subject to formal 'findings of guilt' in courts of law (except perhaps in cases of homicide); and if decisions about their education and treatment were made in consultation with their parents by teachers and social workers who are in daily contact with them in their schools. Nor can I accept the argument that it is contrary to British justice that a child should be 'deprived of his liberty' by being sent to a residential institution without formal court proceedings. To that there are two answers. First, this argument by implication identifies 'residential' with 'penal', and assumes that the child is, as his parents so often express it, to be 'put away'. But, happily, now that approved schools are to be merged into a general system of community homes for *all* children who for whatever reason cannot live with their own families, there will no longer be any specifically penal institutions for children of school age. Secondly, a child cannot be deprived of a liberty which he has not got. Children are not free to choose where they should live or what sort of school they should go to or indeed whether they should go to school at all: some are sent to Eton by their parents, others to secondary modern schools by local authorities: others (until recently) to approved schools by the courts. These are all open institutions from which the child can run away if he is so minded: though to all of them he may be returned by his parents or the authorities, as the case may be. He has no freedom.

Finally, let it be added that these proposals would, in effect, merely extend to all children the treatment normally accorded to those of middle-class parents. It is by no means unknown for public schoolboys to steal, but how often do they figure in the clientele of our juvenile courts?

III

If the penal system can only do too little too late, when the horse has already bolted, what goes wrong as long as he is safely within the stable, and where can we look for remedies? Here I would offer two hypotheses, each of which relates to certain aspects of our contemporary way of life as presented in my opening lecture.

First, let us recall the dramatic decline in religious observance and religious belief that has characterized the twentieth century: the genuinely convinced Christian, who accepts the Gospel story as literal truth, is now extremely rare. Yet we base the moral education of the young on the dogmas of the Christian religion; although it is not always realized that the statutory obligation to include religious instruction and a daily act of worship in the curriculum of every county school dates only from the middle of this increasingly agnostic century. It could indeed be said that the 1944 Education Act was designed to inculcate in children beliefs which their elders were already discarding. Even today the Report of the Church of England's Commission on Religious Education takes back with one hand what it gives with the other. 'To press for acceptance of a particular faith or belief system', its authors declare, is . . . 'certainly not the task of a teacher in a county school', while religious education should be 'acknowledged on educational grounds and not by singling it out and making it alone of all subjects legally compulsory'. Nevertheless it is proposed to retain the 'conscience clauses' in the present legislation which allow teachers to refuse to participate in, and parents to withdraw their children from, religious education and the daily act of worship. But if teachers are not 'pressing for the acceptance of a particular faith', why are these clauses necessary? There are no such provisions for exemption from, say, French or mathematics lessons. Moreover the Commissioners' courage and logic clearly failed them when it came to the formal "act of worship". This, they say, should remain, and will, it is presumed, 'in most county schools continue to be placed within the Christian tradition' – though 'a greater element of flexibility should be allowed . . . than is permitted by existing legislation'.[14]

In the meantime what do we actually teach children as the religion which is to be the basis of their morals? As an example, let us look at the agreed religious syllabus in use in my own county. This certainly makes no bones about its propagandist purpose. 'The aim,' it declares, 'is to secure that children . . . may seek for themselves in Christianity the beliefs and principles which give true purpose to life, true standards of value, and light on the problems, and difficulties of life.' 'In the light of the teaching of Jesus Christ, we shall surely achieve our greatest aim when our pupils become full and practising members of a Christian Church'; and in the syllabus itself it appears that both the virgin birth and the resurrection are taught as historical facts. The evidence for the resurrection, it is said, 'is to be found on every page of the New Testament, for apart from the Resurrection, there would have been no writings, no Gospel, no Church'.[15] Even more remarkable is the inscription written into a Bible that is still presented under an ancient bequest by the County to children who gain a place in their grammar schools. 'The Surrey Education Committee,' this reads, 'present you with this book, the most valuable thing this world affords, desiring that you use it while at school and

---

[14] *The fourth R: Report of the Commission on Religious Education in Schools* (SPCK 1970), pp. 103, 274, 275, 104, 140.
[15] Education Committee, Surrey County Council, *Syllabus of Religious Education*, 1963, pp. 8, 111, 116.

retain it when you leave. Herein is wisdom which will lead you
to all truth, provide comfort and guidance and teach you the
whole duty of man.' If the Bible does indeed contain all truth
and teach the whole duty of man why do we spend money on
the rest of their education? No doubt the original testator
sincerely believed all this; but no intelligent child of today will
swallow such nonsense. Besides, if he does read his Bible, and
includes the Old Testament (which also has a prominent place
in the agreed syllabus) he is more likely to find that, in the
recent words of an eminent physician, this is 'an obscene
chronicle of man's cruelty to man, or worse perhaps, his
cruelty to woman, and of man's selfishness and cupidity,
backed up by his appeal to his god: a horror story if ever there
was one . . .' and 'totally inappropriate to the ethical instruction
of school children'.[16]

That indeed is the point. Inevitably increasing numbers of
children will either critically reject the Christian dogmas as
obvious fairy-stories of highly variable moral value; or, more
probably, they will just disregard the whole business as mean-
ingless and of no relevance to life as they know it – as their
fathers and mothers have done. But the real danger lies in the
fact that it is on these dogmas that current moral teaching is
founded, and on the supernatural sanction which they imply
that it relies for its enforcement. Rejection of the traditional
religious basis of morality thus leaves a dangerous vacuum.
Nor does it help matters that some eminent divines, notably
Dr John Robinson, the former Bishop of Woolwich, while still
retaining the churches' claim to unique positions of power and
privilege, now admit that Christianity as presented in the
churches, in the schools and over the air deserves no credence.
Of all the attitudes which Christians might adopt in face of the

[16] Letter by Lord Platt to *The Times*, March 19, 1970.

incompatibility of their doctrines with common experience and contemporary scientific knowledge, I would have thought that this was the most clearly suicidal, since it merely adds scepticism as to the integrity of the churches' leaders to incredulity as to the truth of what is said in their name.

What is needed to fill the vacuum is a moral system which accepts the fact that the only human experience of which we have certain knowledge is that which falls between birth and death; which invokes no supernatural sanction; and which derives its precepts from the importance of promoting happiness and welfare here on earth. No doubt there would still be those who, for reasons not yet understood, lack the normal human susceptibility to moral conditioning. But can it be doubted that a morality based on the general welfare and happiness would have a better chance of acceptance than one contingent upon the truth of so improbable a story as the incarnation of an omnipotent deity into human form by the conception of a virgin and his subsequent resurrection from the dead? Yet until the opportunities for presentation of such a moral system match those now enjoyed by conventional Christianity the vacuum will remain, and with it the risk that some amongst us may grow to maturity untouched by any morality at all.

That, anyhow, is my first hypothesis as to the increase of anti-social behaviour, particularly in relation to property and violence. My second hypothesis springs directly from the characteristics of our acquisitive and competitive society, as described in my opening lecture. It is a simple hypothesis, and is certainly not original; but it is consistent with the fact that recorded criminality has been increasing for a long time, and that some at least of the most affluent countries of the world are among those in which this increase has been most dramatic. In

an increasingly competitive educational system, from stream-
ing in the primary school, through selection or rejection at
11+ and – for the fortunate few – on through the gates of the
University or technical college, what matters in life, we soon
observe, is to force our way up ladders. Some of us, however,
are born without the brains to master the educational ladders,
while others are handicapped by environmental conditions
which militate against any kind of intellectual exercise. In consequence we are labelled failures even from our earliest school
days; and thus may the seeds of resentment be sown. In the
work-a-day world, again, opportunities for creative and satis-
fying work are few and far between, while the more rewarding
jobs are increasingly barred to those who, though perhaps
competent enough, lack the special ability to acquire paper
qualifications. Professional certificates are required for many
technical posts, but a skilled safe-breaker need pass no exams.

Social expectations have, moreover, also changed. Theoretically, this is the century of the common man, the century in
which all doors are open, and in which it would be thought
wrong to suggest that the Lord God made the rich man in his
castle and the poor man at his gate, or that anyone ought to
accept with resignation the state to which either God or man
may call him. But the theory and the actuality do not match.
If some doors have opened a little wider, others have been
closed. To a vast majority of the population, work today is
merely instrumental in the sense that it is just a means of earning money; and everything everywhere – be it commercial
advertisement, the sight of other people's conspicuous
affluence, or the smash and grab system which governs the
distribution of income – everything, everywhere emphasizes
the supreme importance of having plenty of money to spend.

The past half-century can indeed boast a fine record of

boredom, rejection and cupidity. The cupidity is almost universal and the boredom and rejection widespread; and together they make a fertile soil for theft and vandalism – especially in a world which likes to pretend that all opportunities are open to all. Why were there 35,000 convictions last year for the offence of the unauthorized taking or theft of motor vehicles? Answer: because the use of a car is a source of both prestige and excitement in our culture, particularly to the young male; and these offenders had no cars of their own.

Criminal behaviour is extremely complex and various, and no simple theory comes near to accounting for its many manifestations. My hypotheses can do no more than suggest possible explanations of the supposedly paradoxical coincidence of growing affluence and increasing disrespect for other people's property and persons. Fortunately, if miraculously, most people, most of the time, lead reasonably law-abiding lives. But the ability to tolerate frustration varies greatly as between individuals in virtue both of their genetic constitution and of their environmental experience. Two factors will determine the proportion who at any time will vent their aggression on a society whose demands have become intolerable. The first is the intensity of the frustrations to which they are subjected, and the second is the expectation of the community at large that these frustrations ought nevertheless to be tolerated. My thesis is that both these factors have changed in a direction which contributes to the post-war increase in recorded crimes against persons or property.

IV

The world which I have presented to you is marked by striking contrasts and curious values. It is a world of conspicuous affluence and of less conspicuous miserable poverty. In the matter of personal enrichment, it is totally permissive, and has perversely come to regard the right of the strong to trample upon the weak as a basic democratic freedom. While it is still shackled by prohibitions and taboos which it cannot justify in terms of earthly human welfare, it is gradually coming to believe that morality is no concern of any supernatural being, but must be conceived in purely human terms; and in this way the sum of human misery has certainly been reduced. To those who have enough money (and enough means the middle rather than the top of the hierarchy), and who have some control over their physical environment, this world now offers opportunities of happiness and enjoyment greater perhaps than have ever before been within reach of so many. Yet still the price of this happiness is indifference to the needless frustration and the avoidable hardships endured by millions for whom these delights are legally unattainable. So we end where we began, in the competitive acquisitive society. It is that society which presents the challenge of the future.